To Johandy —

"Art is not a handicraft, it is the transmission of feeling the artist has experienced."
— TOLSTOY

JPrescott
Bud
2015

The OLD MAN

and

HIS DREAMS

A Memoir

LEROY H. (BUD) PRESCOTT

This book is a so-called "fictional" memoir; a memoir is a biography or an account of historical events, especially written from personal knowledge; this is "fictional" because I can't remember everything exactly, and because, sometimes, I may just choose to misremember other things. It is, however, basically and mostly, quite real, and very true to my life.

— LHP

Copyright © 2015 by Leroy H. Prescott

All rights reserved.

No part of this book
may be used without permission
except for purposes of review.

ISBN-13: 978-1515325123
ISBN-10: 1515325121

Other books by this author:

SOUNDS FROM INSIDE ME
A Collection of Poems
PEFERRED EDITION

SOUNDS FROM INSIDE ME
A Collection of Poems
(OUT OF PRINT)

THERE ARE SIRENS IN THE CITY
A Novel

MASTERWORKS 3.0

This book, this life, these dreams, are dedicated to my wife, Arlis Evon Prescott (née Woken), who is, of course, the best of my dreams come true.

The author and ARLIS on the occasion of their 53rd anniversary, August 18, 2015. They are on the <u>Green Line</u> to St. Paul for lunch at <u>Christo's</u> in the <u>Union Depot.</u>

"... your old men shall dream dreams,
And your young men shall see visions."

— The HOLY BIBLE . . . Joel 2:28

– TABLE OF CONTENTS –

Preface	1
Prologue: First Things First	3
1. What the Heck Is a "Fictional" Memoir?	5
2. In the Mean Time, In-Between Times	9
3. So Goes the Show Business	13
4. Lights, Camera, No Action	19
5. Those Who Can; Those Who Can't	23
6. No One's Above (or Beneath) the Law	29
7. The Church Is Most Certainly With Us	33
8. Wow! Look at All the Big Buildings	37
9. Whoever Heard of a Four-Ring Circus?	41
10. It's Not About the Money, or Is It?	49
11. The Other Side of the Coin	53
12. Take Me Here, There, and Anywhere	57
13. I See London, and Then Some	63
14. What if I Were a City?	67
15. Hi, Tubby! Hey, Slim!	97
16. I Shoulda' Coulda' Been	101
17. Who Else Would I Be?	105
18. The Real Me, By the Numbers	109
19. To Sleep, Perchance to Dream	115
20. Some Other Crazy Dreamers	121
21. Reality Is the Other Side of Dreaming	125
22. A Dream List or Two	129
23. What if I Never Dreamed of It at All?	135
24. Never Dreamed It; Couldn't Be Better	141
25. When a Dream That Never Was Comes True	145
26. Was It All Just a Dream?	149
Epilogue: Hey, Dreamer, It's Time to Wake Up	151
Coda	155
Acknowledgments	157
About the Author	159
Bibliography	161

– PREFACE –

WHAT IS IT?

The preface is an introductory part of a text, an introductory section at the beginning of a book or speech that comments on aspects of the text such as the writer's intentions (that's what the Dictionary says).

WHY HAVE IT?

I like the idea of a preface to help set up and to help give direction to the project. It's kind of like the first heading in an outline, the Roman numeral I, which, then, can be followed by as many other sections as needed to organize what is waiting to be said, and each of those sections can have sub-sections and sub-sub-sections until the order and the substance is established. I, also, like the fact that it helps give a book structure and balance (I'm a huge proponent of structure and balance): Title Page, Publishing Information, Dedication, Epigram, Preface, Prologue, Chapters, Epilogue, Coda, Acknowledgements, About the Author, Bibliography, Printing Information.

WHO NEEDS IT?

Obviously, I do. I am setting out, here, to tell something, to tell many things, about myself, and, that sort of frightens me. I am not usually one to share all that much personal stuff. I'm perfectly willing, and, I think, quite generous, when it comes to sharing goods and services; I love doing that; it makes me feel better, and it helps others to feel better, too, but I'm not comfortable sharing too much of what is inside me, what is the *real* me.

It's just that I'm actually a very private person; I'm really rather shy, more so than most people who know me might ever have expected. Now, here I am, preparing to *spill the beans*, to *dive right in*, to *bare my soul* (okay, that may be a bit much), to *turn myself loose*, to *tell all* (or, at least, to tell a part) of who and what and how I am.

I feel a need to be write this memoir, but I, also, feel the need to be careful. I must remember things as best I can; I will have to think before I write; I will have to rewrite and edit; I want to tell it well. On the other hand . . . with all of that in mind, I will beware, and I caution . . . let the reader beware.

– PROLOGUE –

First Things First

Let's just get this out of the way. I was born on June 30, 1937, in a small town in central Minnesota, Princeton, in the closed-in front porch of my grandparent's house situated on a gravel-covered County Road 18 on the north side of town (the wrong side of the Rum River, by the way). It was a very hot, dry, dusty day, and, as my mother often remembered, it got even hotter, and drier, and dustier in the days that followed. She had to be counseled by my grandmother (confirmed by the doctor), not to wrap me so tightly, not to cover me so much; often when I cried, I was just way too hot; babies are even more subject to overheating than adults, and can be in some danger when they are over-protected by a new mother.

Four days later was the 4th of July; we called it Independence Day back then. The town always had a big celebration in those days with a carnival, a parade, fireworks, dancing, and a beer garden. In the past, my mother and my dad had never missed it. They grew up in that town; they went to high school there; they dated and married there; they were in business on Main Street. My dad loved to be where the people were; he was quite the "glad-hander," very social, very well-known, and very popular; he should have been a politician (he did dabble in politics, but he was careless, and it never quite worked out for him). My mother was quite the opposite, rather quiet, relatively shy, much more reserved. She did like the parade; she loved the carnival rides; she marveled at the fireworks; she loved to dance, and . . . she especially enjoyed the beer garden.

Years later, we talked about the fact that she had missed that particular celebration; she was, after all, still recovering from an at-home birth; it was still exceedingly hot and dry and dusty; and, of course, she now had a baby to take care of and . . . to keep cool.

I often wondered if she ever resented my intrusion into her life; if she missed going to that celebration; if she ever dreamed of a different, a more unfettered life. I don't really think so, but we have joked about it over the years. We did really get along well most of the time; she was often my most helpful friend. I am quite sure, however, that what she missed most that year was the dancing and the beer garden; she could dance until dawn, and she surely enjoyed her beer, well into her later years.

We continued to live with my grandparents until my dad moved his café from Main Street to a more roadhouse-like location further north on the same stretch of highway. There was a small apartment in the basement of the new location, and that became my second home.

I think that this is where my imagination came into play, and where I really learned to dream a little, and, then, to dream big. I was alone a lot; my parents were busy upstairs in their business, although they often had me with them. I got to know their customers, and came to feel like a *favored* child. Downstairs, I had lots of toys; I had a good radio, even a phonograph to listen to; I had lots of picture books. I learned to read early, however, so I had lots of other books, too; I came to love books.

There were no neighbor kids around to play with, so I loved it when my cousins came to visit, which wasn't often, but which was always fun. I was alone a lot, but I was not a lonely child; in fact, most of the time, I was quite comfortable being by myself; I would have to say, that, later, when I was involved with my own growing family, with my profession and with other assorted businesses, and with a multitude of social activities, I always relished what time alone I could manage. Frankly . . . I still do.

– CHAPTER ONE –

What the Heck Is a "Fictional" Memoir?

This is not a book I ever intended to write; you can be quite clear about that. Despite my usually outgoing façade, the extroversion I often project, my apparent boldness, I am, actually, a very private person, quite internal, even shy, most uncomfortable when presented, revealed, exposed, and . . . especially protective of who and what and how I really am. A very wise high school teacher of mine described me as the most introverted extrovert she ever knew – or was it the most extroverted introvert?

As it happened, then, during the time I was working on a commissioned biography of a very distinguished and successful individual with an intriguing childhood, a remarkable background, and a delightful personality, I was asked by an often overly-curious person, but a usually quite well-meaning person (and a close personal friend), "So, what about you?"

"What?" "Huh?" That was my immediate, and sort of confused, and rather amused, and really off-hand response. I was quite taken aback. I'd never even considered that. Then . . . after a minute or two, "What about me?"

"When are you going to write an autobiography or, at least, some kind of stories about yourself, about your own *long* and *varied* and *different* and *difficult* and *exciting* and *interesting* and *special* life?" "What?" "Huh?"

It turned out that my friend was not being facetious, and she went on to point out story after story, incident after incident, that I had told or, perhaps, hinted at, over time, about myself; that overly-curious friend, that well-meaning friend, that close friend, actually meant it. "What?" "Huh?"

I suppose it is just possible that I merely imagined (or misremembered) that my friend had actually used all that descriptive stuff about me (*long* . . . for sure; *varied* . . . very; *different* . . . often; *difficult* . . . too much so; *exciting* . . . sometimes; *interesting* . . . highly; and *special* . . . maybe).

Okay, because that friend knew me well enough and had known me long enough to know that there certainly was some truth to be told, maybe, there was a real story to tell.

I thought about it a long time, and, then, I thought about it some more. Was there really a personal story to tell that would be worth someone's taking the time to read? Would anybody else really care?

Somewhere along the line, somehow, I was convinced (or I convinced myself), that maybe there was something worthwhile to tell. So . . . I decided to launch this project: I would do something of a *fictional memoir,* mostly true, but sometimes colored by what I really cared about, and by what I could sort of actually remember. The concept of *fictional memoir* is currently riding a wave of popularity. I'd read several myself; very evocative, very particular, and, often, very interesting.

It is my impression that almost all autobiographies or memoirs are somewhat fictional. Who can really remember the specifics of a conversation, the exact colors of anything from the past, the feelings, the emotions, the myriad of people involved in one's life? Who can recall, then, with any accuracy, the *real* details of a lifetime? It seems to me that what finally gets to the page is what's fondest, what's held one's interest over time, what's most harrowing or difficult, what's recalled by others, or . . . what one really wants to remember. I do have one particular advantage, though; I have kept a journal daily for the last 28 years. I have a lot of it already written down; those pages are in the file (more about that later).

It was decided, then. I would do it. And . . . I was decided that my *"conceit"* would be to use the dreams of a lifetime, of my lifetime, the dreams of this old man, as it were, and that I would tell what I remembered, or what I wanted to remember, or, probably, what I misremembered as well as could be expected of my very personal story.

– CHAPTER TWO –

In the Mean Time, In-Between Times

I was looking for my next project, anyway. I had recently published my first novel, THERE ARE SIRENS IN THE CITY (which contained explicit sex, and murder most foul, and was quite unlike me), and I had already started on its sequel which just wasn't going all that well.

I had turned, then, to gathering together a collection of my many poems, which I, subsequently, published as SOUNDS FROM INSIDE ME (A Collection of Poems), which were accessible to all and dedicated to my six grandchildren. Those poems did, indeed, suggest a lifetime of varied interests and attitudes and directions and experiences. I finished that book in time to give each of the *"grands"* an inscribed and autographed copy for Christmas. Oh, yes, they each also got a bookmark wrapped around a twenty dollar bill, which, it must be said, they seemed to appreciate even more than the poems.

The biography project had fallen through because of some bickering among the participants (a wife, a caregiver, and the subject, himself). I was really disappointed; I liked what I was doing, what I had done so far. I had completed the prologue and four chapters, and those who had already previewed the work were excited about it, too. Then, just like that, meetings were cancelled; calls went unanswered; work just stopped; research materials from a personal collection were withdrawn. I was eventually contacted with one weak explanation and a brief apology. Needless to say, I never saw a cent for the research, for the interest, for the work I had done; that unsatisfied project now lies festering in a file drawer.

I needed another project, and, although, I had never intended to write a book like this, it just kept coming to mind, and the ideas were right there waiting for me; my head was suddenly full of the stuff of my life; apparently, a lot of my dreams were still with me; maybe they did need to be captured and explored; so . . . I started . . . just like that . . . *in medias res* (in the middle of things, as it were) . . . wherever . . . whatever . . . whenever . . . why-ever . . . and so . . . away we go.

Many years ago, I wrote the lyrics to a musical called CHILDREN OF ADAM, CHILDREN OF EVE; my son, Rick, wrote the music. It was never produced, only workshopped, but those who heard it, loved it. Later, it was entered in a project aimed at developing new work; it was the runner-up. The title comes from a section of Walt Whitman's LEAVES OF GRASS; Whitman is a favorite of mine, and our songs were about different kinds of people and different aspects of life and lives just as many of his poems were; they are a series of musical character sketches.

I guess these favorite lyrics from that show foreshadow this book:

THE DREAMS OF A LIFETIME

All my lifetime
I am dreaming,
Dreaming of the
Days gone past;
Dreaming of the
Good times coming,
Coming to me,
Here, at last.

In the Mean Time, In-Between Times

All my lifetime
I am trying,
Trying to be
Something more,
Every day a
Little better,
Better than the
Day before.

All my lifetime
I am wishing,
Wishing wishes
Would come true;
Wanting to be
Moving onward;
Upward is the
Thing to do.

I am wishing.
I am trying.
I am dreaming,
So are you.

A beautiful woman,
The handsomest man,
An elegant townhouse,
A velvet divan,
The dreams of a lifetime
Must be better than.

The OLD MAN and HIS DREAMS

A silver streak limo,
An emerald ring,
A magnum of champagne,
The crown of a king,
The dreams of a lifetime
Are some other thing.

A dream of a lifetime
Is having a friend;
It's laughing together;
Good health without end.
A dream of a lifetime:
Some daughters and sons,
The sweetness of sunshine,
While happiness runs.

A dream of a lifetime:
Your spouse by your side,
Some chance to imagine,
A smile ever wide.
A dream of a lifetime:
A spirit that soars;
My dream of a lifetime:
That you should have yours!

Keep on wishing.
Keep on trying.
Keep on dreaming . . .
The dreams of a lifetime.

These, then, letter after letter, word after word, line after line, paragraph after paragraph, page after page, chapter after chapter, are the dreams after dreams of this old man's lifetime . . . so far.

– CHAPTER THREE –

So Goes the Show Business

I always dreamed of being in some kind of show business. I love everything about it. My passion was for the stage rather than for movies or even for TV, but I knew that I would take whatever came along. I've always loved the movies, though, and I've seen, quite literally, hundreds of them over the years; and I do love TV; I have always watched shows regularly and faithfully (I once was a coder for a media research company, and my area of expertise was TV). If I'm honest, I probably have watched TV way too often and way too much.

I might choose to be a great playwright, a TONY award-winner, a PULITZER PRIZE-winner, a truly successful one, of a musical with a message which transcends mere entertainment, or of serious plays with honest characters and with real heart. I might be satisfied being an award-winning actor if I could play major roles in Shakespeare's plays or sing the lead roles in a hit musicals, but that is really a second or third choice.

My passion? I love to direct. I have directed many high school and community theater and summer stock plays and musicals. I like the idea of taking something from *"scratch,"* from the printed page, and putting my ideas, my special touches to it, to bring it, literally, to life. Of course, I would really love to direct in the *"big time"* on Broadway or for significant major repertory houses around the country. I often imagine doing what I have done with little or no budget with a big enough budget to really be reckoned with.

Of course, I dreamed of making a living at it, of becoming successful, of becoming wealthy, and of becoming famous. That was the dream . . . ah . . . yes . . . but . . . then . . . there is always the reality!

This is the reality: I wanted to direct THE MIRACLE WORKER as a high school senior class play, but when I inquired about it, I found that it was not yet available, so, quite disappointed, I searched for something else appropriate for the class I was working with. Then, out of a clear, blue sky, I was contacted by the releasing company asking whether I would want us to be one of five high schools in five different parts of the country to premiere the play at that level. Of course, I jumped at the chance, and two months later, we opened. I think it was the first time ever that a class play was the featured component of a pep fest, and everybody cheered when we read a telegram from the <u>Foundation for the Blind,</u> on behalf of Helen Keller, whose growing-up was the subject of the play, telling us to "Break a leg!"

Here's some more reality: I was directing for a summer stock theater in central Minnesota; I had moved there for the summer to be better available and to be able to manage the elements of the production. On the first night of technical rehearsal, there was a glitch in making a lighting change, so I called a halt and told the stagehand that I would come on stage from the orchestra pit, show him how it should be done, and, then, we would just continue. I went on stage; I made the adjustment; it worked well; everyone now knew how it was supposed to be done; I headed back to my spot. As I did, I called up to the light booth in the back that we were going right on, so he could just kill the lights. I headed for the edge of the stage; the lighting technician did just as directed; and I, now in total darkness, missed the steps and plunged into the orchestra pit, five feet below, and all concrete. My only thought as I was falling was, "This is really gonna' hurt!"

And . . . it really did! But, we had to get a show on, so I called out to bring the lights up, and we continued. It was not until after the scene that anyone knew that I was even hurt, and it was not until after the show opened (my having continued to get it ready while in much pain, and probably in shock) that I discovered that I had broken my right leg and torn all the muscles and ligaments and whatever else there was from ankle to behind the knee. I was a full year recovering from that little adventure, but I was true to the philosophy (or was it the folly?) that the show must go on. That, dear readers, is the real show business.

Again, I refer to my original musical review, CHILDREN OF ADAM, CHILDREN OF EVE; the review is a series of what are essentially musical character sketches. My son wrote the terrific music to what I think are some often clever and sometimes really pithy or poignant lyrics. It never did get produced, but it did have a preview presentation which was much fun, and was very well received; sometime later, it was the runner-up in a competition for new shows to be work-shopped for production by a major regional theater. We got to see the production of the winning entry. Perhaps you can remember the old saying, "We was robbed!" Well . . . <u>We WAS robbed!</u>

This lyric from that show sort of sums up my whole show business dream (I wrote the part essentially about me and, hopefully, for me to play):

> I want to be in show business.
> I want to take a shot.
> I want that toe-to-toe business;
> Want to be hot, yes,
> I want to be hot!

> I want to be In show business.
> I want to do real well.
> I want that vo-de-oh business;
> Want to do swell, yes,
> I want to do swell!

> I want to be in show business.
> I want to be a star.
> I want that give-and-go business;
> Want to go far, yes,
> I want to go far!

I've said earlier that being an actor was a second choice, at best, but I have acted many times, and I find that it has many of its own satisfactions. Acting is difficult! Acting is work! It takes as much time as talent, and it takes even more energy. It requires one to leave oneself behind, backstage or in the wings, to inhabit somebody else for a period of time, and that somebody may be quite different from you, the actor.

I find the hardest part to be learning lines; I'm something of a purist, and I want to get the lines exactly right. I work intensely when I have to learn a role. I copy out the lines on index cards (which I always carry with me even into the performances). I work mostly on my own with full concentration, no distraction allowed, but I also can work with someone else to cue me, to feed me the lines, someone to react and to react to. I, once, played the role of the Villain in a Melodrama, FOR HER CHE-ILD'S SAKE; I had 750 "sides" (a side is one speech, no matter how short or how long); I spent hours at learning that part; it was presented by the faculty in New Prague, where I was teaching at the time, as a fund-raiser for the arts program; I certainly didn't want to screw that up; after all, I was an English, Speech, and Drama teacher, and Department Chair. I spent hours and hours on those lines; I always do. I do not like *"going up"* on my lines; I have only rarely done it; it is oh-sooooo embarrassing!

Once, I said someone else's lines before he got the chance to end the play; he looked at me in such a way that I realized what I had done, so I said my own lines and we went on. In his turn, he paused, looked intently at me and said my lines before he turned to the audience, smirked, and proclaimed his end-lines with a flourish while I cowered upstage as far as I could get.

I do love the camaraderie of an acting company. Over the years, I have made great friends with many of my fellow actors. I love to go see them in other productions, and I love it when they come to see me in another role. I love the traditions, too, like saying, "Break a leg!" for good luck rather than tempting the fates with the real thing. There is a tradition of no whistling backstage; it doesn't really apply to me, though, because I'm tongue-tied and just can't whistle.

Once in a production of "The Scottish Play," all the members of that particular cast agreed to break the tradition of never saying the play's real name in the theater except on stage. We all decided, instead, to shout and repeat "MACBETH!" for energy and for challenge before each and every performance (there really were some who were quite hesitant). As it turned out, we had great fun; we got great reviews; we ended up being a sell-out; we were only seriously troubled one time by a major snowstorm which caused us to cancel a performance. The cast of that show chose, once in awhile, to award a black rose to a cast member who had contributed particular energy and who had made a difference to the show; I am lucky enough to have received that rose.

I don't especially like wearing costumes; I once wore the perfect pair of purple high-heeled boots for a part as a king, but they did not fit very well, and they left my feet with bruises, blisters, and raw sores; as I put it, they practically *"killed"* my feet. I don't mind wearing makeup; I'm pretty good at applying it to myself and to others. There is that element of artistry in getting the right look just right. I once made up my brother to look older for a Halloween party, so carefully, so exactly, so precisely, that photos of him compared to photos of our dad looked to be the same person.

The irony, in regard to the costumes, is that for 6 years I was a professional costumer, managing several costume houses, traveling from coast to coast, and dressing hundreds of shows. Once upon a time (that's how most fairy tales start, and this seemed like a fairy tale to me), I was recognized as the leading *"from-stock"* costumer in the country, and, as such, I was "coaxed" away (I suppose "hired away" would do just as well) by a competitor to accomplish the merger of the two most famous New York costumers, and to do work for the Broadway stage. I must admit that I was very flattered, almost giddy, but I managed to negotiate an excellent contract, with a good salary, an unlimited travel allowance, unlimited prime show tickets, a generous expense account, and a rather nice place to live. After all, a good business head is also good show business.

Oh, yes, and I think it needs be said, throughout that whole experience, I was always treated very well with kindness, with courtesy, with deference, with dignity, and with style.

– CHAPTER FOUR –

Lights, Camera, No Action

I never wanted to be in movies, although I have, literally, seen hundreds of them over the years. I love the movies; I especially liked the old MGM and 20th Century Fox musicals, and I loved the epics adapted from the BIBLE, and those about mythology, about the other Gods, and about the heroes of old.

What I dreamed about, however, in regard to the movies, was the celebrity. I wanted to be a celebrity; I wanted to be a star! I wanted the fame; I wanted people to recognize me, to look up to me, to treat me in special ways. I wanted the success; I wanted the advantage of having proved myself; I wanted to be honored, even revered. I also wanted the fortune; who doesn't dream of the prospects from wealth? I can read my ego at work here . . . I . . . I . . . I . . . I . . . I . . . ay . . . ay . . . ay . . . yay . . . yay. Okay . . . it's time to move on.

The movie stars had mansions on hills and in gated communities, and there were servants; the movie stars wore fine clothes, designer clothes, well cut and a good fit, and there were dressers; the movie stars had fine cars, stretch limos, Porsches and Ferraris, and there were drivers.

That was the dream . . . the dream . . . the dream . . . "Cut!" Bang . . . clatter . . . crash . . . ring . . . ring . . . ring . . . "Cut!' And . . . one awakes to the reality.

My biggest house was in a good location, had three stories, and a winding stairway, and there were many more rooms than we needed; there was a long driveway leading to an attached garage;

however . . . the house was old, and ramshackle, weather-worn, and it badly needed paint, but . . . the rent was cheap. On one occasion, a very strong winter wind blew out a pane of glass in a vacant upstairs room, and left us freezing from the below zero temperatures and the cold breeze until we hunted it down and boarded it up with plywood. And then there was the ghost; was there one or wasn't there? I always say "she" was there; don't ask me why "she"; it just seemed like a "she." My more practical wife says "Get serious," or "Serious up!" as we always phrase it. But . . . what about the shuffling footsteps down the long hall and climbing up and down the stairs? What about the little voice sometimes calling softly, sighing, soughing? What about the door to an area we weren't supposed to use which was so often ajar?

We never talked about it with the kids, but we once overheard part of a brief, huddled conversation where the subject was quickly changed when we were spotted. They weren't scared at all, just very curious. We thought we were keeping it from them, and they thought they were keeping it from us.

I always tried to dress well and to keep up with the fashions of the time; I bought good clothes, but I had to fight for a good fit because of my weird build (long legs, too much middle, and thin neck). Imagine, then, the shock to the conservative community where I was teaching and where we lived when I showed up at a very formal school event in a turquoise-colored tuxedo jacket, black slacks with a side-stripe, a black turtle-neck shirt, and a large lavaliere. The kids loved it; their more conservative parents were not so sure. Those were the days, my friends. Those were *"those"* days.

The first car I ever owned was a second-hand Buick Riviera hardtop; I loved that car; My dad had always driven a Buick, but never one as "cool" as this one; he had helped me pick it out and had helped me pay for it. The best car I ever owned was a silver Mercury Marquis, all tricked out and really quite elegant. I once bought Arlis a <u>Mercury Topaz</u> for her birthday on her birthday. The finest car I ever drove (a perk with my job) was a forest-green <u>Lincoln Mark IV</u> that got 10-12 miles to the gallon on the highway, and I was commuting 50 miles one way to work each weekday; premium gas was around $1.50–1.80; I still couldn't afford it. My favorite car was a rust-colored <u>Mercury Montego</u>, which all my sons used in learning to drive; it's most serious problem except for *real* rust in its later years, was a collision with a deer; the deer did not survive; that had to be reported to the DNR; the damaged <u>Montego</u> and the shaken driver did survive; that had to be reported to Mom and Dad.

Once I started driving (which was later in life than most young people), I drove a lot; Some years I drove 40,000 miles back and forth to work; I sort of enjoyed that time alone in the car where it could act as a compression chamber to help set me up for the day ahead, and a decompression chamber to bring me back down from the stress and strain of a difficult work day. I pride myself on not swearing, but sometimes my language seriously deteriorated, in a sort of road rage, but contained inside my car, on that long drive home.

Of course, I was the driver; I never, ever had a driver. Now, however, when I no longer drive because of my health, I'm pleased to say that my gracious wife (who has always loved to drive and who once tried out for a "powder-puff" derby at the hometown stock-car track where my dad was the announcer) is my regular chauffer. So, away we continue to go.

– CHAPTER FIVE –

Those Who Can; Those Who Can't

Did I ever dream of becoming a teacher? I don't think I ever did. Did I really want to be a teacher? I'm not at all sure that I did. Was it just sort of inevitable that I would become a teacher, because everyone else thought I could and should and would be one? Now that is entirely possible. And . . . I did . . . of course . . .after a stint studying Psychology . . . end up becoming a teacher.

I majored in Speech and Theater at the <u>University of Minnesota</u> where I got my <u>Bachelor of Science Degree</u>. The required minor in those days for that particular major was English, so that one would actually have something *"worthwhile"* to teach when one got out into the real world and into real schools. I actually have an *extended* minor, because I took so many extra English courses, just not always the right ones to qualify for that major. Eventually I took graduate courses in several academic areas from different sources on and off campus in order to keep moving up to the next level on the faculty salary schedule; hence, it turns out, that I also have a Master's *"equivalent"* (again, enough courses, just not always the right ones to qualify, and . . . I never did write a thesis). If I had it to do over, I would get that done; it's one of my biggest regrets.

I did teach for several years in public high schools; I taught mostly seniors, and . . . of course . . . I taught mostly English. I loved much of what I taught. I loved the early English classic, BEOWULF (circa 900 A.D.):

> . . . *gewitan meahton*
> *idese onlicnaes; other earm-sceapen*
> *on weres waestmum*

wraec-lastas traed,
nefne he waes mara
thonne aenig man other;
thone on gear-dagum
Grendel nemdo(n)
fold-buende . . .

Or, if you prefer:

One of them seemed,
so far as folk could fairly judge,
of womankind;
and one, accursed,
in man's guise
trod the misery-track
of exile,
though huger than human bulk,
Grendel in days long gone
they named him,
folk of the land . . .

The seniors in one high school had rather inelegant nicknames for virtually all of the teachers: one very nice man, who was rather stout with no neck and who had a somewhat hooked nose, was called *"Rhino;"* another was called *"Blower,"* because he talked a lot and mostly just loved to hear himself whether anyone else did or not. I remember that there was a *"Doofus,"* (which just means "dumb;" and actually seemed so appropriate), an *"Assassin"* (for all the close-to-right reasons), and a *"Miss Priss,"* (so prim and so proper, just too good to be true). Behind my back, I was called *"Grendel"* after that monster from BEOWULF. Hey, I made sure that it was kept in check and behind my back, but I never minded that. Why should I? I was actually kind of flattered. Methinks, along the way, I just might have taught somebody something.

I love Geoffrey Chaucer's CANTERBURY TALES:

> *Whan that Aprille with his shoures sote*
> *The droghte of Marche hath perced to the rote,*
> *And bathed every veyne in swich licour . . .*

Oh how I love the sound of the Middle English of those lines from the Prologue, and, then, of course, how I enjoy all those wonderful stories. I like Chaucer enough that our second son's middle name is Geoffrey.

I love William Shakespeare's plays; they were a major part of my teaching and theater careers. Who doesn't recognize these lines from HAMLET?

> *To be, or not to be: that is the question:*
> *Whether 'tis nobler in the mind to suffer*
> *the slings and arrows of outrageous fortune,*
> *Or to take arms against a sea of troubles,*
> *And by opposing, end them?---To die:---to sleep;*
> *No more;*

And, later, in that same speech, ". . . *to sleep: perchance to dream . . .*"?

I have two favorites among the 37 plays, MACBETH and THE TEMPEST. I am well-acquainted with the former; I taught it to high school seniors each winter 4 times a day for 8 years; I've seen it many times on stage and in the movies; and . . . at the age of 70, I played the Thane of Ross with a talented Shakespearean company in what just happened to be my very first contracted and paid acting experience; the key words here: *"contracted"* and *"paid"*. Some of my very favorite lines are from MACBETH:

> *To-morrow, and to-morrow, and to-morrow,*
> *Creeps in this petty pace from day to day,*
> *To the last syllable of recorded time;*
> *And all our yesterdays have lighted fools*

the way to dusty death. Out, out, brief candle!
Life's but a walking shadow, a poor player,
That struts and frets his hour upon the stage,
And then is heard no more; it is a tale
Told by an idiot, full of sound and fury,
Signifying nothing.

I have used that speech, which Macbeth uses to ponder, ever so briefly, in the midst of the turmoil going on around him, his wife's suicide (*"She should have died hereafter . . ."*) as an audition piece. And . . . I have used those words to inform a dramatic and serious poem, "Tales of Sound and Fury," which can be found in my collection of poems, SOUNDS FROM INSIDE ME.

I have seen THE TEMPEST on stage many times as well; I have also made the effort to see it in its many presentations, especially in the movies. Crazy as it sounds, I still have plans to produce it someday; I've analyzed it and shaped it, and know exactly how it should be done (read: "how I think it should be done"). I wonder how many others over the years have said the same thing about this play or about their own favorites. Of course, at one time I wanted to play the main character of Prospero; sadly, I'm very past that prime, now; it's a big part. Prospero is an exile; he is driven by revenge; he is strong; he is a wizard, a magician; he is also a loving father, and, many people think that he is, in fact, the very embodiment of Shakespeare himself. For all his rage, his hurt, his efforts in revenge (he creates the storm, he comes to control his adversaries, he engineers the relationships, he does it his way), he is truly magnanimous and benevolent; imagine that in a power position.

I had a successful teaching career; I met and worked with many wonderful teachers. I was the Chair of the <u>Language Arts Department</u> for many years, and I was active in the teachers' organizations at local, regional, and state levels. I also had many wonderful students; many have gone on to be teachers. There are always some you like better than others, but the "others" are few and far between; not very many have landed in jail.

I have fond memories of classroom projects that went above and beyond what students can or will normally do; I asked much of my students. There was the building of a working catapult demonstrated in the school's courtyard; the making of an exact scale model of Shakespeare's <u>Globe Theater</u> which is still on display; mentoring a class of younger students who needed those more mature role models to let them know that all this school stuff was worth it; writing, as a group effort, a complete novel about Medieval times, as long lost now as are those times; creating and performing an all-school lyceum program which had to keep the other students laughing rather than throwing things, we succeeded in not being *"lame"*, which is a major compliment.

I may have forgotten to mention the building of a small-scale but working guillotine also demonstrated in the school's courtyard on assorted vegetables. What about the simulating of an opium den as from a Sherlock Holmes story they had read? And, then, there was the making of a somewhat risqué movie that was really quite good, but which definitely had to be re-edited for a mixed and proper audience.

We learn something from everything we do, and from everyone we meet; that's the hope, and that's a good thing if we will make the best of it. Teachers and students do that for each other; it's a give and take. Teaching others should be the dream of many; teachers can be both the professional ones and the other mentors in our lives. We really need good teachers, starting with good parents.

Learning, on the other hand, should be the dream of everyone, and, in that, we need to continue to be dreamers, and we never want to give up on that dream.

– CHAPTER SIX –

No One's Above (or Beneath) the Law

I never actually dreamed of being a lawyer; that was my dad's dream for me, or rather, for him. He often lived on the edge, challenging, pushing back against, questioning, contradicting how things were. And . . . he had a big, successful business which needed more of a certain kind of attention than he was able to give. His hope was that, someday he could turn the advocating side, the organizing side, the controlling side, the practical side of that business over to me to manage. He, then, would be free to do the promoting side, the prospecting side, the marketing side, the fun side, and the imagining side. Ah, yes, you can see that he was a dreamer, too, and . . . sometimes . . . sadly . . . he just couldn't get beyond that.

I wouldn't have minded being an attorney. I don't mind representing people. I am an organized, detail-oriented person. I have a performer's demeanor. I am a good speaker. I think I present myself well. In high school, I participated in Debate and Mock Trials and Model Legislature. They say that it is not bragging when it's the truth; I usually won!

I have advocated for others all my life (especially for students, and, of course, for other teachers); I have stood up for their causes and rights. Once, even, I was threatened with jail time by the School Board's negotiator in the face of standing strong for teachers' rights; I wasn't arrested; I wasn't jailed; it was really just a rather scary threat. We fiercely stood our ground, and we won our point.

I am well-organized; I keep my home and personal effects in good order (we have filing cabinets, and business boxes, and other labeled drawers), mostly for convenience, but, sometimes, just for the fun of it. It's true that I do alphabetize my shirts and trousers by color on the closet rod (dark blue comes before light blue), and, it is also true, that my socks are stacked in the sock drawer by season, by color, and by ankle, calf, or knee. We are not even going into my underwear drawer.

Of course, I'm a performer, and I can turn on the style and manner needed at the turn of a phrase or by the attitude or approach of another. I was a speech teacher, so I think that I know the rudiments of communicating with others while getting my ideas across and understanding theirs. I recited the <u>Gettysburg Address</u> annually at Lincoln's Birthday celebrations when I was in grade school. I was, perhaps, the shortest, tubbiest, non-bearded Lincoln-portrayer ever in a church play (which was about his younger years as narrated by his older self). I was a serious declamation student and a regular participant; as a senior in high school I was runner-up to the state in the "Original Oratory" section; in my speech I was advocating for improved care and treatment of our mentally ill. That speech was published in more than one local paper or journal; it was described as strong, even strident, but also thoughtful, touching, poignant, and . . . heartbreaking.

I stand tall; I carry myself with dignity and pride; I hold my head high even if I don't feel quite that way (remember that I am, sometimes, an actor and a pretty good one, who may have to play a role whether he feels that way or not). I have always taken pride in how I looked, not in the vanity sense, but in the sense that I am representing myself, and my family, and my friends in a way that can reflect well on them, too; I like good clothes and just the right look.

I wouldn't have minded being an attorney. I have always wanted a nice corner office of my own (don't they all have them?). I would love to have had a secretary or personal assistant (I once did have a secretary in another business situation; she was so efficient; I loved it; I could always get so much more than just the usual accomplished.

I like the idea of others seeking me out for help; I am always willing to help if I can. I could even entertain the prospect of that training and experience leading to other things. Could I have been a politician? That would have been another of my dad's dreams for me. It was, certainly, a part of his dreams for himself. I do not even have that inkling, although I have held several elected positions at lower levels; I was elected to many offices including class president twice and twice to the Student Council.

I'm not sure what it was that turned me off to actually pursuing a law career. Maybe it was that external persistence and pressure, when, in fact, I was listening to my own internal persistence that I wanted to be something else; I was listening to some other of my dreams.

I think it's worth mentioning, though, that I love John Grisham's books; I've read all of them (except those for young people, which I'm going to get to); they immerse me in both the dramatic and the mundane elements of the law and of people's lives; they are about causes and about what's right. It is also worth mentioning that one of my favorite TV shows of all time was L. A. LAW; a friend and I would watch it separately each week, and then get together the next day to go over the stories, the characters (what a fine ensemble of actors), and the details; we never did quite get over that dramatic and devastating fall one unpleasant character took into an open elevator shaft, but we were satisfied that Rosalind Shays was gone.

– CHAPTER SEVEN –

The Church Is Most Certainly With Us

I did imagine myself as a pastor. I sort of continue to do so even though I feel too old and really too past my prime. It would have been an unlikely and rather ironic choice for me, since I was the son of an agnostic bartender. It's an interesting footnote to my story, though, because my dad had a thorough understanding of the BIBLE; he had read it completely off and on and more than once over the years; and he could argue for or against its positions and practices with anyone and everyone if they so chose; he liked to play *"Devil's Advocate."*

He surely practiced the "Golden Rule" to the extreme; we often had a guest at our supper table, or on the back steps with a sandwich and a cup of coffee, or in our spare room, or on a couch in the attic for the night. There was always someone picking up some yard work or making some porch repairs or repainting the kitchen or the pantry whether they needed it or not. No one in need ever went away empty-handed, and friends and relatives could count on his support for any and every cause, especially their own. When he died, we found page after page of signed documents and IOU's never collected, nor, indeed, ever even asked for.

I remember his inviting in the Mormon missionary pairs of young men who regularly came through town; he would offer them cold water if it was hot out, or cocoa if it was cold, and a snack if such seemed needed, and he would take the time to talk with them (he was home days, because his business was at night), never shooing them away or shrugging them off. I'm sure there were times when they questioned his theology, or rolled their eyes at his lack of a traditional spiritual belief, or wondered what they had gotten themselves into, but they always listened to him, and questioned or answered, and . . . they often came back another time or two just to chat.

I remember the Methodist pastor stopping by to check on my involvement in the church (my mother was raised Methodist), and his ending up staying for hours to discuss and debate with my dad this, that, and whatever. I went regularly to Sunday School; that was important to my mother who had been raised rather strictly. I participated in Christmas pageants, junior choir, trips to visit and perform for "seniors" in nursing homes and for other social groups, and the youth fellowship.

When it came time to be confirmed (actually a bit after the usual age), I helped organized a group of friends to take the classes together, and we had a great time both in the fun and in the learning what it was all about. We lucked out with a great pastor/mentor who kept us all in it together until we had accomplished what we set out to do. I remember that I got my first "grownup" sport coat and a new tie to go with my gray dress slacks to wear to the confirmation ceremony. I also remember that I had not yet been baptized, because my parents were unchurched at the time, so that was combined with this significant part of my coming of age.

I have always felt that my faith journey was in my own hands. Once determined to stay on it, being the obsessive-compulsive kind of person I am, I have never wavered from it. Oh, it has changed direction sometimes; I went from Methodism to Lutheranism when I married a died-in-the-wool Norwegian Lutheran. I have changed churches over the years, not willing to be tied to location or certain direction or attitude, but I have stayed active. We have even had the privilege of helping to start a new congregation where I was the first Council Secretary and was responsible for developing the church's library. I have served on several other church councils and have held different offices; I've been participant in more-than-one delegate assembly; I've taught Sunday School and even superintended; And . . . I've preached on several occasions when a lay leader was needed to do so, and . . . I've loved it.

One of my favorite "sermons" was called "Fight the Good fight . . . of the Faith" which compared the so-called "Industrial Revolution" with the times in which we now live. It was not unreasonable to quote Charles Dickens from A TALE OF TWO CITIES:

> It was the best of times, it was the worst of times, it was the age of wisdom, it was the age of foolishness, it was the epoch of belief, it was the epoch of incredulity, it was the season of Light, it was the season of Darkness, it was the spring of hope, it was the winter of despair, we had everything before us, we had nothing behind us, we were all going direct to Heaven, we were all going direct the other way.

So . . . the reality is . . . I have had bits and pieces of opportunities to be or try to be a reverend, a pastor, a preacher, an engaged lay person, a serious student of the church, a teacher of the faith, and a dedicated Christian. Does that dream still live on? Hmm . . . maybe . . . just maybe . . . it does.

– CHAPTER EIGHT –

Wow! Look at All the Big Buildings

I love buildings: big ones, small ones, short ones, tall ones, crooked ones, straight ones, old ones, new ones. I have eclectic tastes when it comes to buildings; I love 'em all. I should have been an architect. I'm a designer of other things, and I have played at designing buildings for years just drawing them for fun. One of my favorite shop classes was the mechanical drawing section; my drawings were neat and careful and exact and perfect (if I do say so myself); it's the first shop class where I ever got an "A". We're not even going to say any more than this about my arc-welding.

I could never have been a builder; I admire them for all the things they can do that I can't even come close to; my brother got those skills from somewhere; he is a master of his trade. My grandfather was a serious carpenter, but he would take on any hare-brained project, so we called him a "jackknife carpenter." I have built or rebuilt different things over the years including the finishing of a full basement, but, although I eventually get it right, it takes me too long, and I never have exactly the right tools (or, perhaps, the patience).

I have designed and built in many other media. I've used modeling clay to build whole villages that were stored under my bed as they continued to grow and collect dust. I've used <u>Lincoln Logs</u> and <u>Tinker Toys</u> to construct cabins and amusement park rides and for weird experiments. Imagine, then, the thrill of discovering <u>Legos</u>. I have built building after building with those little bricks; our kids did, too; our grandkids do now. We still have the hundreds of those blocks that our kids grew up with, and the grandkids love to build with them when they visit, but they build so much better.

I've made hundreds of scale drawings of theaters, especially, trying to get the perfect one; but I also like drawing school buildings (they were a part of my life for so long), and shopping centers (don't ask me why, although I was a part of the advertising project for <u>Southdale</u>, the first indoor shopping mall).

I always take the time to examine the architecture whenever and wherever I visit; sometimes I admire it; sometimes I criticize it; sometimes I love it; sometimes I hate it. Whatever . . . I am delighted to be observing it, and I am glad that it is there.

Of course, I have favorites. I love the whole <u>Rockefeller Center</u> complex with those promenades, and the fountains, and the ice rink in winter, and the statue of "Prometheus." I've visited that complex several times (actually, inside and out); I've been to the top of "30 Rock," one of my favorite views of the city, especially at night. I also love <u>Radio City Music Hall</u> just across the street; we've seen several shows there and have had the backstage/behind-the-scenes tour, and even met some of the "Rockettes".

By contrast, I've been all over the <u>Trump Tower</u>, and I find that it has its own appeal, such extravagance, such expensive "cheap" chic, such fun. On our bedroom wall in a collection of favorite paintings and pictures; among them is a framed photo of our reflections in the mirrors that surround those gilt escalators. I must admit that I almost removed this choice; recently Donald Trump has been in the news for mostly the wrong reasons; but this chapter is about architecture, not politics, so, I left it in.

I love <u>Westminster Abbey</u>. I was in awe of its size and scope, its solidness and its durability, but what I really appreciated were the tombs, or memorial spaces, dedicated to the great writers, politicians, and royalty of England; I liked the way it all sort of fit together. I felt that it was a solemn space, but oh-so awesome; I was quite overwhelmed (except for the oh-so-touristy gift shop by the front door).

I'm intrigued by the buildings that climb high in the sky. I've been to the top of the Empire State Building and to the top of what were the World Trade Center towers (on a windy day, mind you). We are sorry for the loss, and we will miss them. In Chicago, we've been up in the Hancock Building and what was the Sears Tower (I'm not sure what it's called now). I like it up high looking down, but I like it just as much looking up.

I've never been to the Pentagon, but I marvel at what I know about its size and its labyrinthine interior; we can understand its importance to us by the attack on it on 9/11; we can marvel at how soon it was put back together. We should also marvel at the importance of what goes on inside there.

My favorite castle (everyone needs to have a favorite castle) is Warwick Castle on the Avon River in central England. I love its long, broad, flat wall which allows no access with that sheer drop to the river's banks. I love its grounds which are maintained nicely to satisfy tourists, but which reflect its real time and place with lots of artifacts scattered about. I've climbed the towers just to get the feel of what it was like; it was narrow, winding, tight, uncomfortable (just like going up in the Statue of Liberty). I wanted to look out at the surrounding countryside (it's an agricultural area with quaint gardens and broad fields and small picturesque villages). I've descended into the deepest and smallest of its dungeons, and I was so enthralled by the old and rusted weapons of torture on display, and by the very darkness and by the palpable dankness, that I quite forgot to be claustrophobic.

It doesn't just have to be something big. I have admired the "mushroom cottages" in Northern Michigan, so nicely nestled in the perfect glade, so rustic, so fairytale-like, so . . . cute. The day we were there was a rather dreary day, sort of misty, and there was a light haze hanging over that whole development, just as it really should always be.

It doesn't even have to be a building for me to admire it architecturally and design-wise; I enjoy seeing the new, the different, the parts of the whole. Have you ever been to Branson, MO, and gone to the bathroom in Shoji's theater? You need to go there just to go. I've been in more elegant ones in much different and better and finer places, but I have never been in one that was more extravagant; there was actually a grand piano in the foyer. I have to admit, and I'm not ashamed to, that I loved it.

– CHAPTER NINE –

Whoever Heard of a Four-Ring Circus?

– RING A –

A POEM ABOUT THE CIRCUS

A feeble clown,
A dirt-streaked truck,
A horse, a pair, a herd.

An elephant,
A ticket booth,
A tent, a breeze, a bird.

A wire high,
A swing, a rope,
Some cotton candy, too.

A camel, dust,
A barker tough,
A special thing to do.

A circus . . . live,
A stop in town,
A day, a night of joy.

A circus . . . live;
Who is a man
Is once again . . . a boy.

– RING B –

DON'T YOU JUST LOVE IT?

Does anyone else even remember "TOBY TYLER or Ten Weeks with a Circus"? It was published in serial form in 1877, then published as a book in 1881. It was popular for years. I can assure you that I did not discover it in its earlier appearances, but I enjoyed reading it when I did.

I thought, as I started to write this, that I remembered the book (I clearly remembered a boy and a circus), but when I looked it up in order to refer to it here, I discovered that it is not at all what I remembered. Over the years I had romanticized it, when, in fact, it was meant, in its time, to teach a lesson to recalcitrant children. Toby was a 10-year-old orphan who ran away from a dreadful foster home to join the circus which he, too, romanticized when it came to town. What he discovered was an even more difficult life than he had known: hard work, not enough food, being cold, whippings, loneliness, all with his only companion and friend, a chimp.

Wow, that's not at all where I planned to go with this chapter; that side of the circus, the deeper, darker side, will just have to wait for another teller of tales, or . . . it can just stay at rest with Toby Tyler.

I love the circus; I always have, and when I was an adolescent, I dreamed of joining one the first chance I could; I wasn't exactly going to run away, you see, but I wanted to get involved, maybe just for a summer or two. I, literally, took every opportunity that came my way to get to know what circuses were all about. What was it that I wanted to be or do? I've tried rope-walking (low to the ground); I've swung on trapezes (even upside down); I've tried to train my own dogs to do tricks on command (with little luck). I really don't know exactly what I wanted to do; maybe I could have been a sideshow barker, or . . . yes . . . that's it . . . a Ringmaster.

I have seen many, many circuses; I once, in my maturity, crawled up to (actually was helped up to) the very best level of some rickety bleachers on one of the hottest summer days when I had a broken leg and a 40-pound fiberglass cast from foot to hip. I just couldn't miss that experience, that opportunity, even this one time. As it turned out, it was a delight; the popcorn and lemonade were good, and it was some good therapy for me after being laid up all summer.

I have been front row, center ring, where the horses could kneel directly to me and to my family; where the dancers could bow and swirl close enough to touch; where the clowns were in our faces cajoling and teasing us; where the popcorn and peanuts and cotton candy never tasted better.

Who doesn't remember, at least hearing about, Ringling Brothers Barnum and Bailey Circus: "The Greatest Show On Earth"? I can assure you, I remember it well; We saw its centennial edition, the blue group. So, I say: been there; done that. Not enough said for sure, but . . . maybe . . . just enough said!

I also remember: Clyde Beatty, Carson and Barnes, the Cole Brothers, Circus Vargas, the Miller Brothers, and Al G. Kelly (Millers and Kelly eventually merged just to stay competitive). And who does not recognize the ubiquitous Cirque de Soleil? In fact, one of my favorite Las Vegas shows is "Zumanity", a Cirque de Soleil production which I found to have all the finer elements of a circus (I laughed, I cried, I almost wet my pants), but which was even more lavishly produced, was even more side-splittingly funny, and was quite seriously and most deliciously X-rated. I saw it on my 75th birthday with my wife, who was teased and cajoled by this smooth, suave, sort of nasty MC to join the show for the evening; she declined. When we saw the show, we seriously blushed at what would have been her part . . . OMG . . . enough said!

– RING C –

"FIRST OF MAY," WHAT SAY?

I think I was about 13, the summer between junior high and senior high. I had seen the posters all over town "The Circus Is Coming!" with drawings of big top tents and wild animals and clowns, and with stickers across the bottom that asked for "local help." I had talked to my parents about that, I wanted to be one of that "local help." We knew others from town, kids mostly, but several others who were not otherwise seriously employed who wanted or needed the work; they would be at the "grounds" bright and early the day of the show to pick up a few extra bucks, maybe a free lunch, and/or passes for the family for that night's performance. It was often a case of *"the early bird gets the worm,"* with jobs available to the locals right then and now.

The jobs were not just menial, especially in the hot sun and the humidity of a mid-summer day; there was hard work to be done: heavy pulling and lifting was needed helping to set up the big (or little) "Top" and the tents for the sideshows and the concessions; there was feeding the animals and cleaning their cages (of you know what); there was running errands all over town if something special was needed (like mechanical parts where something had broken, extra feed especially when the hay was low, or hawking tickets downtown to help fill the house).

The "grounds" on a normal day were/was just a large vacant lot across from the public utilities building, catty-corner from the train depot, and side by side with the potato warehouses. The advantage of that space was that the land was big enough and was flat enough with well-worn-down grass already gone to brown;

another advantage was the trunk highway passing by on one side, so any event would definitely be noticed; there was plenty of parking on side streets in the nearby neighborhoods, and there was another extra lot across the street the other way that could accommodate more vehicles.

I got to the "grounds" late, much later than too many others; I was not an *"early bird,"* there might not be a *"worm"* for me. I had waited until my dad was ready to take me and to drop me off, so that he could check out and be satisfied with the situation. I could easily have biked (or even walked), but that's not how we usually did things; it needed to be checked out and determined to be safe and worthwhile.

As it turned out, though, I did get a job that day, a hard one but a fun one (it may have had something to do with an acquaintance who was already working there). In one's first season working for the circus, one is called "First of May" because that's when the season kicks off; it has come to mean that the worker is new and raw and vulnerable, easy to threaten, and fun to tease, and, here I was, for sure, "First of May" (a *real* "rube"). My job . . . how truly glorious . . . was to . . . I pause to catch my breath . . . I can still feel the thrill of it . . . feed, care for, and clean up after . . . believe it or not . . . the . . . elephant. There was only one elephant, and not a very big one at that, but she became my responsibility for the day.

Probably, I need to talk more about this particular circus; it was small . . . very small . . . just one-ring; it could set up in a day, play a late afternoon and evening performance, strike the whole set, and move on in the night to the next town. We called these circuses "dog and pony shows," because those animals made up most of the acts: cute costumes, tandem riding, obstacle courses, counting, and catching various things. There were human acts, too, of course: a slack-rope walker, a low-flying trapeze artist, a family of jugglers, assorted acrobats, and many different clowns. Oh, there might be one or two wilder animals, as well: a tired, mangy-looking lion or tiger, a baboon or a chimpanzee on a leash, a cage full of monkeys, a donkey, a python or a boa constrictor, a trained pig, and, once in awhile, as in this case, a small elephant.

The elephant's name was "Dolly," and . . . she knew her name; she responded to it if and when she wanted to, which was not always; she seemed to like to be called by name, though. I would have to say that she also had a sense of humor and/or a real playfulness; there seemed to be a twinkle in her eyes. She was tethered on the shady side of her truck to a large stake by a huge chain with a leather cuff; she could move around quite easily, but only in a circle; she never lay down while I was there, but she could if she wanted to.

I enjoyed my late morning and early afternoon with her. I dragged heavy straw bails from the feed truck, broke them apart, and spread them for her to eat and to kick around. I used a rake, to keep the area tidy, and I used a shovel, more than once, to clean up the area and to follow up on one particularly aromatic and definitely very large dump for such a small beast. Dolly turned her head, raised her trunk, and opened her mouth after she deposited that load as if to smirk at me for what she had just done and, now, was making me do.

I talked to her as I worked with her, and I sang; she seemed to like the songs, especially "I've been workin' on the railroad all the live long day . . ." and "You are my sunshine, my only sunshine . . ." and she seemed to respond to other remarks, comments or suggestions; she would definitely move around for me, as I sprayed her with a hose (she loved that) and as I scrubbed her with a large, hard, broom-like brush (not loved so much).

The last thing I did before I left for the day was to fill her trough with fresh, cold water, stroke her trunk, and tell her how much I had enjoyed our day together, and that I would see her that night at the show. She did seem sort of sad, her trunk was hanging down, her eyes were not wanting to look at me, or, perhaps, I just imagined that, because I was feeling sort of sad, myself. As I turned away to go to the car for my ride home, and just as I looked back one more time to wave, she let out a small "trumpet" and, then, she blasted me from her trunkful of fresh, cold water. She had perfect aim; I got soaked. Oh, yes, Dolly, my friend(-for-a-day), you made sure that I would never forget you, and I haven't. I was there the night of the show; I'd like to believe that Dolly remembered me when she saw me as she paraded by; she did seem to be smiling.

– RING D –

THE CIRCUS TRAIN

Are you crying, little master?
Are you crying?
Is there reason
For your cheeks so damp and wan?

Yes, I'm crying, dearest father;
Yes I'm crying.
For the circus train was here
And now is gone.

I was happy
For a moment, dearest father;
And my cheeks were bright
And rosy with my smile.

You'll be happy
Soon again, my little master.
Dare I say
Before the train has gone a mile
Dare I say
Before the train has gone a mile.

– CHAPTER TEN –

It's Not About the Money, or Is It?

I have always dreamed of being rich! There, I've said it. I've owned up to it. I've proclaimed it to the world (or, at least to any and all who read this book). I know it's crass; let's be quite clear about that: CRASS . . . so thoughtless, vulgar, and insensitive as to lack all refinement or delicacy (that's according to Webster).

I've had some taste of what it is like to live with uncommon wealth. We were not always poor to middle class. The family business was quite successful; my dad owned and operated one of the largest ballrooms and supper clubs in central Minnesota; we appreciated the finer things in life (well, if not appreciated, at least we enjoyed them).

I remember the time when my parents were going on a trip to Chicago for business and pleasure; my mother needed some new clothes; their shopping trip yielded five of the finest couture dresses available in the nearest best shops, as well as several pairs of shoes and some handbags. Oh, yes, and just to top off everything else, because, after all it was winter, and Chicago is really cold with that wind blowing off the Lake, there was an elegant full-length fur coat. And for my dad, the finest Harris Tweed, double-breasted, belted, full-length overcoat. Why not? We could afford it.

Times changed, however, the big business failed; playing politics on the wrong side of the county officials had a lot to do with that. Too much money had been spent along the way, much had been lent, some just thrown away, and not enough had been saved for a rainy day. The slide was painful; my dad never recovered. I dreamed of being rich . . . richer . . . richest, again, someday. But . . . then . . . there is the reality.

I had the experience of spending many summers with an aunt and uncle who were rich, indeed, and whose fortune had never waned (is it more delicate to say "wealthy" or "well-to-do"?). My mother's oldest sister had married a promising, young surgeon (she had been his office assistant), who worked hard at it, was good at what he did, and was well-liked; he fulfilled and realized and maintained that promise. He rose steadily in the ranks of his profession to being the one to go to; he became Dean of an important medical school, and he was renowned world-wide in his particular specialty, Scoliosis. He was invited by the Shah of Iran to develop medical programs for, what was then, a rich and emerging country.

They had no children of their own, so they delighted in having me and two of my cousins (we were the same age) spend time with them. They treated us well, buying us toys and clothes and special treats. They took us places: to the movies, to the "real" theater, to sporting events, to parades and carnivals and circuses; we went swimming at private beaches, and boating on fine yachts; we dined out at the finest and most elegant restaurants. Along the way, they taught us how to act, how to present ourselves well, how to look just right, how to represent them. I thrived on that, I loved it, and I got the most frequent opportunity. To say that I was the favorite might be a stretch of my imagination, but I did spend most of the summers and the longer school holidays with them while I was growing up, those most impressionable years.

My one cousin was sickly; he had been born with a heart defect; he was just not always up for too much activity and too much new adventure, so he had to give up on those summers, which could be exhausting. He was one of my earliest and dearest friends; we were so much alike, and I missed his being there with us, just I miss his being around to this day. He died from one of the earliest open-heart surgeries, because, frankly, we just didn't know as much about it then as we do now.

My other cousin was very shy, rather quiet, and could never quite get used to the significant differences from his own simple home life and such an active social scene. I spent a lot of time with him as we were growing up; he was my second-best friend; as it is now, we have gone our separate ways, and we seldom see each other. I was supposed to be his best man when he married; unfortunately, I missed my bus connection to home and to the wedding after a layover for repairs and a changed schedule; that didn't exactly keep me in good stead, especially with his new wife, but we all moved on, and we remain friends.

These, then, are the memories and the dreams; the reality is something quite different. I've never been even close to being rich again, try as hard as I might. I've been successful and comfortable to be sure, but we've stayed pretty much between the poor and the middle-classes, or, maybe, between the middle and the upper-middle classes; but who's counting or categorizing? Oh, that's right, I guess I am (that's what this chapter is all about), so I'll have to admit something else . . . I'm still working on that rich . . . richer . . . richest thing; but . . . I am beginning to tire.

– CHAPTER ELEVEN –

The Other Side of the Coin

Being rich, wealthy, well-to-do, better off than others, comes with an obligation; at least in our family it did. My grandmother would have been a Baroness if the family lands and the family fortune in Prussia had not been confiscated by the Germans in the wake of two world wars. What was left was a handful of letters documenting what was, what should have been, and what was no longer. It's a sad story, from another time, for too many people, but there was this one thing left in the family that came down through the generations to me.

Noblesse oblige is the idea that people born into the nobility or to the upper social classes or to wealth must behave in an honorable, generous way toward the less privileged. It's a simple enough idea, but . . . its implications can be profound. I am a product of that idea in a somewhat more realistic way than I might be if the family wealth had been maintained, but . . . our family obligation was, nonetheless, to help others in any way we could, to make things better for other people.

Let's start with my grandmother, who took the concept quite seriously, quite literally, and who practiced it regularly and wholeheartedly. My grandparents did not suffer the indignities and the serious difficulties that so many did during the Great Depression. They were lucky; they had a good business, but, even better than that, they were good money managers; they had seriously saved for a rainy day. Because of this they felt the obligation to assist others, to clothe them if needed, to get them around to where they needed to go, to give them a place to stay, and, certainly, to feed them. It was said of my grandmother that she set a dinner table so that if another whole family needed to join them, there was more than enough food to go around. Truth be told . . . it happened more than once, and there always was.

My grandfather was a Dodge and Plymouth dealer; so my grandmother always drove the newest model Dodge; she loved her car, and she used it to squire friends, neighbors, relatives, even total strangers around the town to doctor's appointments, for grocery shopping, to parties and picnics, to work where there was some, and to church on Sundays even though she, herself, was not a regular church-goer.

Needless to say, she was beloved (and that's not just rhetoric). I adored her; she had helped raise me when my parents were busy establishing and maintaining their business; we had even lived with them for awhile (remember, I was born on their front porch). I also adored her cooking, especially her apple turnover, which is just like it sounds, a cake on one side and apples on the other, serve it right-side up, or upside-down, either way it was delicious.

My dad, the oldest surviving son (his older brother had died young of food poisoning), inherited many of the same qualities; he was very close to his mother always (years later, when she was seriously ill as a result of diabetes and a major car accident, he helped to nurse her back to the best health possible). His business was successful, and he felt the need to share what he had, to help where he could, to be there for others. When he died, we found ledgers and notebooks and boxes full of IOU's, scrap after scrap, name after name, column after column, page after page; some were marked "paid" in long hand; some were just scratched through; most of them had just lingered there for years, and had never been repaid, actually thousands of dollars worth (from a time when a dollar was worth something).

It was not uncommon for my dad to give someone a job, not because he needed something done, but because someone needed a job, a decent meal, some dignity. It was not uncommon for my dad to give someone a place to sleep; we had an old daybed in an attic space off my bedroom, and I remember waking up late at night as someone was escorted to a decent place to sleep, and/or waking up early to the surprise that there was, indeed, someone snoring just behind that attic door. Did someone need groceries: a friend, a neighbor, a relative, a new acquaintance? My dad would take them shopping, or just buy some staples (bread, milk, butter, eggs, cheese) and take what was needed to those in need.

It was not right, not proper, to ask back for what one had done or given, so there were no particular rewards in doing good deeds, just the doing of the deeds, itself. What was right, was right. Our family, which bore some noble blood, demonstrated in so many ways what *Noblesse oblige* was really all about, and . . . we were never that much the worse for wear.

I have tried to keep up the good work. *"Tried"* is the operative word here. I am one to look at my failures, and wish I had done more, or done differently, or, certainly, done better. We are regular donors to several causes, especially those which might not receive the attention of deeper pockets, or those which aren't very high profile; it's just a part of what we do on a regular basis, not just as we are able. We feel an obligation, but a willing one for sure.

One of our special interests is a church agency that offers all kinds of services to a variety of people in need. It has used furniture available. It has racks and shelves of clothing. It has a well-stocked food shelf. This agency can provide a little cash if needed. It has phone cards available. It even offers health and legal services. It is like a "mini-mall" for those who don't always have the advantage of that kind of shopping. We are careful to supply new as well as used, better rather than barely, and extra cash that is nobody else's business. We are pleased that it is a serious part of our church's ministry. We support it and advocate for it. It makes us feel good.

Of course, we always try to start with family; if we can help when needed, we do; I must admit that we do not always feel appreciated there. We think of that as just the way things are, and we will continue what we can when we can. We have our own list of IOU's that have not been repaid, and there have been times when we could have used that loan paid back into our budget. We try to go into helping others with our eyes open, but, sometimes, it's with blinders on.

We remember some very satisfying transactions. We love paying back, but we love paying things forward even more. When someone has done something for us without expecting anything in return, we make a point of, at least, doing something special for someone else who is in need or might just need extra attention. We love to surprise others with a small gift, a visit, an outing, a card or letter, some delicious baked treats (my wife is known far and wide for her prize-winning cookies). We enjoy making something of a birthday that would not get celebrated otherwise. Come to think about it, it's all about the people, the other people.

We make a point of acknowledging different ethnic holidays, and we love to celebrate them with those who are native to them; who doesn't enjoy margaritas and chips with guacamole on Cinco de Mayo? What about cream cheese wontons and egg foo young, anytime, but especially at the Chinese New Year. Have you ever sat down to a Seder? Have you been to a Bar Mitzvah? Do you enjoy bagels and lox? Have you come to understand that the Scandinavians love lefse, but, also eat . . . I know . . . it's hard to believe . . . lutefisk? Do you appreciate the loveliness and history of a Mass?

We love to try it all, to share with others, when we can, to get to know them, to better understand them. It works the other way to; we reveal something of ourselves, so we can help them come to understand us. I think that sharing of ourselves, as well as our gifts, is some kind of special obligation of everyone, nobility or not.

– CHAPTER TWELVE –

Take Me Here, There, and Anywhere

I have always dreamed of traveling, not just traveling in general (actually, I'm not all that excited about all of the negatives of being away from home, on someone else's schedule, spending money that could probably be put to better use, with a limited selection of clean socks and underwear), but I've dreamed of traveling to specific places. I've been making a list of places I'd like to visit, and checking it twice, or three times, or more, for all these many years.

I think my wanderlust started in grade school (that's what we called it back then), when I was able to select from the junior high section of the library, because I was an advanced reader, and had literally read all of the "kids" section, often sitting there in my spare time reading from one book to another. We could only ever take out two books at a time, and they had to be approved by the librarian. For some reason, I started in the geography section with a book about my home state and another one about South America; don't ask me why; I remember that it was brown, but that it had an appealing picture on the cover of <u>Copacabana Beach</u> in Rio de Janeiro.

I ended up taking that book out so many times (for two weeks each time) that when a newer edition THE OTHER AMERICA (I think it was called) went on the shelves, the older book was given to me to keep for good. I especially loved the section on Brazil, and even more so the sub-section about Rio de Janeiro. It sounded like a fantasy land to me, like nothing I had ever even imagined or even dreamed of, and the photos of the mountains, and the beaches, and the architecture, and the slums, and the beautiful people (who spoke Portuguese, for goodness sake, in a continent of Spanish-speaking people), and the exotic *carnaval* scenes just drew me in. I planned to go there some day; I really wanted to go there; I dreamed of going there; my favorite geography book would be my guide.

That library book is long gone; I don't even remember what happened to it; it was really quite worn out anyway; and it just got lost in life's shuffle. My life has taken its own twists and other turns and gone in so many different directions; none of them has led me to South America; none of them have led me to Rio de Janeiro; I've never been to *carnaval*.

I did get to Mexico once, on a field trip with a school group of advanced students who were taking their senior social studies in Spanish; they were great kids (one of them was our middle son). We visited places in the out-country where the indigenous people didn't even speak Spanish; they spoke Tarascan and hid from us until we demonstrated that we were friendly; we were lucky enough to have a resident of nearby Morelia with us who could sort of help us to communicate.

On Easter Sunday, we took a bus on a side trip from Mexico City to visit the Pyramids of the Sun and the Moon and to see the popular light show at Teotihuacan about 30 miles northeast of Mexico City. We were assured that as late as it would get, there would be busses to return us to the city; there . . . were . . . not! We had to hike through farm fields to a main highway, and we had to flag down a bus to get us back to the city. That bus driver was returning from his long day's trip and bringing a late supper to his invalid mother; as it turned out, he was grateful for the generous fare we offered him, and we were even more grateful to him as evidenced by the more than generous tip the students collected among themselves. And . . . by the way . . . along the way . . . I stepped in a hole and seriously sprained my ankle.

Take Me Here, There, and Anywhere

I've have continued to read about Brazil and about Rio; I still want to go to *carnaval*. I was especially fascinated when Brasilia was established and was built as the new capital way out there in the jungle; that project was a combination of my many of interests: the architecture, the politics, the economics, and the adventure.

I have often dreamed of going to Australia. A friend of mine, who plays the lottery when the jackpot gets really big, has promised me that when he wins, he will send me and my wife to Australia first class and round trip if we prefer. He will surely do that, too . . . when . . . and/or . . . if . . . he ever wins.

I am especially taken with the similarities, the parallels, if you will, of Australia and the United States. I am fascinated with the history, as I have come to understand it, of that huge continent/country, and I am, at this distance, overwhelmed by the romanticism that shrouds that history. I suppose we have our own mystery and romanticism in America; but it is lost on me in the ongoing reality that is so inescapable.

But Australia . . . who wouldn't want to take a trek in the "Outback"? Who wouldn't want to see <u>Ayer's Rock</u>? Who wouldn't want to experience the <u>Great Barrier Reef</u>? Who doesn't think kangaroos, wallabies, dingoes, koalas, and platypuses are much more exotic than moose, deer, coyotes, raccoons, and just plain ducks? Oh, I know the old saying, "The grass is always greener on the other side of the fence." It is all in the perspective, of course, but I want to jump that proverbial fence sometime just to see for myself what's on the other side.

Oh . . . and don't forget that I've read THE THORN BIRDS by Colleen McCullough, and loved every minute of it; I read it late into the night even when I had to be up very early to get to work. I was sorry when it ended. On the other hand, we might just as well forget the fact (although I assure you that I never can), that I saw the first three exciting episodes of the TV mini-series, then left on a major field trip (the one to Mexico, actually), and have never seen the fourth and final episode. I need to locate that episode and finish what I started and had really enjoyed up to a point. I also need to go to Australia, sometime, to satisfy my dream.

Where else have I dreamed of traveling? I've not yet been to New Orleans, nor Washington, D.C., nor San Francisco, nor dozens of other cities in these United States that I would still love to see; I still may try to realize some of those dreams. I do plan to visit San Francisco soon for research purposes; it happens to be the setting of my next book.

I have been to San Antonio several times; one of our sons went to college there. I love it there; I love the <u>Riverwalk</u>; I love the mercados (markets); I like their zoo with that large, angry gorilla who threw something really quite gross directly at me. I have eaten several great donuts from the variety store just down and across the street from the Alamo; I've even been back there more than one time. I was there on the Fourth of July during Texas' sesquicentennial year with my wife, my mother, and 250,000 of our closest and craziest acquaintances, to watch the fabulous fireworks display in the heavens above and around the Alamo. Whiz . . . Pop . . . Bang, Bang, Bang . . . Wow!

We lived in Florida for several years when we became empty-nesters. I went there for a job, which didn't actually work out, because of some difficult associates, but we stayed, because we liked it there. Who knew? We liked the weather, 88-92, that's about all there is to the regular forecast. We loved living as comfortably unclothed as we could, but we carried sweaters in the car to have with us in malls and theaters. We loved the beach; we were there as often as we could be; I will never forget a Christmas Day at our favorite beach with families camped out enjoying their traditional dinners on blankets on the sand and an appearance by Santa Claus. We still think about going back, maybe sooner rather than later.

We are here in cold-winter Minnesota, though, because we have 3 sons, 3 daughters-in-law, 6 grandchildren, and 3 step-grandchildren within a half hour of us. We feel the need of all those birthdays, soccer games, concerts, holiday celebrations, fund-raisers, etc., but, especially, we need those smiling faces and those generous hugs.

I've never been to Paris, not to Rome, nor to the Scandinavian countries; I'm not sure any of those are still in the hopper. I just no longer care to fly, not so much because of the height or the distance, I've never minded that, but because of what one has to go through just to get on a plane, and because of what one has to go through once on board, too much security and too little civility.

I used to fly on business, in the days of dressing properly; of wider aisles and roomier seats; of conveniently stowing away/checking the luggage; of friendly, courteous, even, sometimes, elegant service; of Champagne flights and good food. I do love "First Class"; I've flown it several times; it's expensive, but is the only way to fly!

We flew to Las Vegas (oh, yes, I love that city, too) to celebrate my 75th birthday; we left 2 days before, and we flew home two days after. When I left home, I was only 74, so I had to remove my shoes and jacket in addition to all the rest of the lines and buckets and other rigmarole; when we returned home, however, there were still the lines and the buckets for the stuff from one's pockets, but . . . at 75 . . . I no longer had to remove my shoes or jacket. At that age, I just must have turned into a much better person, and, without a doubt, I was decidedly more mature.

– CHAPTER THIRTEEN –

I See London, and Then Some

I did get to London. In fact, I got, pretty much, all over England. I loved that trip. It came about quite unexpectedly, but it made a dream come true. My wife sang with a church choir which every second or third year made a concert trip to some interesting (usually foreign) place; that interesting place this particular year was to *"merrye olde"* England. And . . . they were looking for a spouse to fill one of the still available seats and to act as a videographer, if possible. Hey . . . look . . . it's me . . . over here . . . see my hand . . . waving . . . I can do that . . . please! And I really could, and I really did. Way to go! I got to go!

We landed in London at Heathrow, but we didn't get to be at all touristy there, just then. We were whisked off to our busses by our tour guide (who turned out to be terrific), and headed for Brighton for the day and for our first night. It is usual to keep going that first day to get used to the time difference and to the jet lag. Brighton was a perfect place to start; it's on the southern coast, on the English Channel; we loved the black sand (or was it small pebbles) beach, and the long and busy amusement pier; we loved the lovely and/or unique and/or expensive homes built along the boardwalk and up on the hills beyond. We were able to have lunch with the daughter of some good friends from when we lived in Florida; the father was from England, and the mother is a decided Anglophile; the daughter was now studying in her father's homeland, living and working in Brighton.

Along the way (no order here, just the experiences), we were in Winchester (yes, we visited that famous Winchester Cathedral of pop song); we were at Stonehenge (where I forgot to turn the

– 63 –

camera off and captured just about all of the walkway around it); in Cambridge we watched the locals "punting" (that's a kind of boating) on the <u>Cam River</u>, and visited <u>King's College;</u> and we dallied in the Cotswolds. It was there, in a very small village, Nether Wallop, which we walked around to see its quaintness, its thatched roofs, and its beautiful rose gardens, that I chatted with a fellow traveler, and learned, much to our amazement, that she was the widow of my high school English teacher; it is not a cliché; it is, indeed, a small world after all.

We stayed a night in Stratford, the home town of William Shakespeare; our hotel was catty-corner from the school he had gone to, and across the street from where his manor home, <u>New Place</u>, once stood. Of, course we trod the boards of Shakespeare's birthplace, and we strolled in the quaint and lovely gardens. Was I dreaming? No . . . this was real. In the very early morning, we wandered down to the Avon River to see the swans, to marvel at riverboat life, and just to soak up the atmosphere. There was a soft breeze and a slight haze; it was calm and serene; we hearkened back to another time, but loved being there in this time.

I was able to attend a play by Shakespeare at the <u>Royal Shakespeare Theatre</u>; MUCH ADO ABOUT NOTHING was done in the style that Shakespeare would, himself, have done, on a spare stage with superb actors. Was I dreaming? No, it felt like being in a dream, but . . . this was real . . . and . . . this was one of the thrills of a lifetime!

We were in Salisbury (one of my favorite books of all time is SARUM by Edward Rutherfurd about this very Salisbury plain); the choir sang concerts along the way and just reverberated in those select surroundings; at <u>Salisbury Cathedral</u>, the organist with us played a concert never to be forgotten. We were at York (by now, we were way far north), where we walked completely around that huge <u>Yorkminster</u> which was forever undergoing years of serious repair. We visited <u>Castle Howard</u> where the PBS series,

BRIDESHEAD REVISITED, was filmed; and we visited Warwick Castle (one of my special choices of architecture), where we literally crawled into that cramped space that once was the dungeon, and where we marveled at the sheer drop of one high, long fortress-like wall that fell to the banks of the River Avon far below.

Back in London, we stayed at the Sherlock Holmes Hotel on Baker Street, just down a couple of blocks from Sherlock's *purported* home. We took a tour of the city; we visited Westminster Abbey; we had high tea at the "Orangerie" (in Kensington Palace, then, the home of Prince Charles and Diana); we had another high tea at Selfridge's (a department store second only to Harrod's, which we also visited, and where I bought the book, LONDON, newly released, and by one of my favorite authors, the aforementioned Edward Rutherfurd).

One night, we went to the London Palladium to see the musical, OLIVER, with real English lads playing the orphans (how right it seemed), and with Barry Humphries, otherwise know as "Dame Edna," an internationally-known Australian comic, playing an endearing Fagin.

One day we walked all over the city, very tiring, but satisfying, to really get the feel of it, and to find the best fish and chips shop and a "pint"; we found a good one opposite Hyde Park just up from "Poets' Corner." We visited a flea market where we chatted with the locals, who were as curious about us as we were about them. We also had the experience of almost being arrested in Hyde Park near the "Peter Pan" statue, just because we were there at that particular time, and because there was some kind of nefarious activity going on nearby. Every one was being stopped, actually rounded up, questioned, and sometimes, even, searched. We were not really very concerned; we were more just curious and excited, and once the "Bobbies" heard our responses, they quickly realized that we were not the ones involved, partly because we just looked and sounded so American touristy.

What we were involved in, though, was a memorable trip to a place we really wanted to see and to get to know. We loved it there, even the food (especially the so-called "country breakfasts") which so often is maligned.

I got some great video; I try not to remember the camera pointed at the ground all around Stonehenge and the too-much coverage of the train museum in York (which was particularly meant for our grandson). I was eventually able to have the trip footage copied into a VHS package of wonderful memories for all. My wife collected other kinds of materials for several scrapbooks (that practice is one of her "things") that could certainly win awards for their style, their thoroughness, their care, their attention to detail, and their specific recollection of a dream fulfilled, a dream to be forever remembered.

– CHAPTER FOURTEEN –

WHAT IF I WERE A CITY?

– PART A –

NYC AND ME (FOREVER)

The dreams about New York City are always with me, and, I think, always have been. No . . . I don't ♥ New York, which is the oh-so-popular cliché version of how people feel about the place; I call it the oh-so-touristy version. It's deeper than that for me, more intense, quite earnest, almost tactile. I feel a kinship with that city, like I really belong there. It should be noted that I did not get there until 1971, but it should also be noted, that we have been back many, many times. I subscribe to the Sunday New York Times, and to New York magazine, so that I can sort of keep up with what is, as I think of it, my city.

However, when I actually did belong there for awhile, living and working, I discovered that my dreams of NYC had me taking it strictly on my terms and not on its, when it should be the other way around. How ironic; how disappointing. It's a strong place, a rough and tough place for strong people; it's a rough and tough place, a strong place for rough and tough people (sic). I have no choice, then, but to assign those descriptions to me, as well.

Let it be said that when I refer to NYC, I mean Manhattan, for the most part. That's where I usually go, but I have been to the other 4 boroughs as well (Brooklyn, Queens, Bronx, and Staten Island). The boroughs were once counties which became these governmental units when they were consolidated as the city.

I once had business in Brooklyn, and, afterwards, my wife and I were taken to an extra fine lunch in what turned out to be a very stereotypical *mob* restaurant, where we were consciously and considerately seated with our backs to the walls, not to the doors, and where everything was ordered for us in courses (a lot of which we did not like).

I once was taken on a wild ride through Queens by a very old female driver who was hell-bent on getting to the meat market before it closed to get the *perfect* brisket (she was teaching her daughter-in-law how to make it just right), but who had to point out all of the sites along the way (we just *had* to see Flushing Meadow), and who had no respect for rush-hour traffic or any particular law.

I was in the Bronx to see Yankee Stadium, of course; I never did see a game there, but it was an icon that needed to be observed and examined. I have been back to see the new Yankee Stadium, which is really right next door, and is big and beautiful, but is just not the same. Oh yes, I also had a frustrating ride through the Bronx to a warehouse to collect props and costumes; the driver this time was young, new to the city, and overly cautious; it took us twice as long as was really needed, because of the frequent wrong turns, and because so much of what we could see looked all the same to us.

Of course, we've taken the Staten Island Ferry from Whitehall Terminal in Manhattan to St. George Terminal on the Island; it's free and only about a 25-minute ride one-way. What a way to travel, daily, once or twice for many commuters; what breathtaking views, especially looking back at the city; what an experience; I love boat rides of all kinds, anyway.

In September of 1987, I wrote a series of short essays about NYC. I'm not sure what prompted them, but it was during the time that I was laid up with a 40-pound fiberglass cast on a seriously shattered leg, and I was looking for something to pass the time of day. Maybe I was missing the city, and was wanting to go back; maybe I had been there recently and was recalling how much fun it had been, and how I felt; maybe I was planning another trip; or, maybe, I was inadvertently laying the groundwork for a sometime book like this one; maybe . . . I was just daydreaming again. I am including those pages here, with only minimal editing, in hopes of showing how and why I ever and always feel the way that I do.

– PART B –

ME AND NYC (THEN AND NOW)

- September 18, 1987 -

I know I am not the only person in the world who feels as I do, but because I feel as I do, I need to set it down. I do not ♥ NY as the popular bumper stickers, posters, and other assorted tourist paraphernalia proclaim. No . . . I just love that city. It was love from afar for a long time, and then love at first sight, and then absence makes the heart grow fonder, and then "love divine all loves excelling" (that's from an old church hymn; perhaps I do go a bit too far, but you get the point).

What is it about this city which prompts such strong feelings, both negative and positive in the visitor? And, what is it about this city that causes people to stay? I choose to explore New York to provide some answers to the questions, at least, as they pertain to me.

My first visit to the city was on a clear, bright, sunny, summer Sunday afternoon. We landed at <u>LaGuardia</u>, which was, in itself, a thrill, and, because of some advance investigation through friends who had been there, caught a bus to Midtown Manhattan, thus saving several dollars in what is, of course, one of the most expensive cities in the world. The ride was hot, and smelly, and bumpy, and slow, and . . . beautiful. I loved being there.

NOTES FROM LATER:

- My wife and I first went to NYC in 1971, then, again, the very next year; after that it became a quite regular vacation or business destination.

- We most often landed at <u>LaGuardia</u> (which is an in-close airport, and, as such, is even a bit scary with its sharply banked landings); only twice have we flown in or out of <u>JFK</u>, and we have never even been to <u>NEWARK</u>.

- I only took a taxi one time, years later, as a time-convenience, when I needed to get to the airport in a hurry; I've used all other kinds of ground and underground transportation. We will never forget the long, late-night subway ride from Queens back into Manhattan with some very questionable fellow passengers.

- One of my biggest surprises on first arrival was the huge cemeteries on the borders of <u>LaGuardia</u> just on the outskirts of the city which lined most of the way from the airport.

- September 19, 1987 -

Even on a hot summer Sunday, the streets in the <u>Times Square</u> area were teeming. The matinees were just getting out, and the lines for the movie theaters were long, and, of course, there are just a lot of people there in the first place. I loved the excitement generated by the people and by the things to do.

We stayed at a venerable, old hotel, the <u>Taft</u>, which for as long as we knew it, was in the process of remodeling its 1500 rooms and its public areas. That remodeling, as such, was never completed; the last time I visited the hotel it was being rehabbed into a cooperative.

On later trips we stayed several times at the <u>Abbey-Victoria</u> just across the street from the <u>Taft</u>. We loved that hotel which was actually a combination of two adjacent properties. The large crystal chandelier in the small, but ornate, waiting area was lovely; the paneled reception lobby was just "right"; and the people were always so friendly. The adjacent café was fine for breakfast, if a bit brusque, New York-style, and very foreign, personnel-wise; their cheesecake was as good as I've had anywhere else in the city. We also had a fine evening in the "better" restaurant at the <u>A-V</u>, an Irish pub, whose name I've forgotten, but whose atmosphere and population felt like the real Manhattan, and whose "Manhattans" went down real good (or, if you prefer, really well) . . . Unfortunately, the <u>Abbey-Victoria</u> is gone now, too, in favor of another high-rise office building.

NOTES FROM LATER:

- I love "Manhattans", especially in Manhattan. One of the best I ever had was at <u>Wolfgang Puck's</u> during happy hour; we were served up with some wonderful home made chips, and the very best of friendly and attentive service; this was one of our all-time highlights.

- We have since stayed at the <u>Edison</u>, the <u>Wellington</u>, the <u>Roger Smith</u>, the <u>Holiday Inn</u>, the <u>Paramount</u>, to name a few.

- I've tried cheesecake, a favorite of mine, all over Midtown; I like it very dense and not too sweet, New York style, and, maybe, with some strawberries. There is something, though, about having it at <u>Sardi's</u> that makes it taste that much better.

- September 20, 1987 -

There was so much to see and do in New York, and things were so expensive that we decided early-on not to waste time or money on eating, at least on eating fancy or fine. We learned to have a good breakfast (usually an inexpensive meal) before even venturing out for the day. If we wanted a really good meal, we learned to have it during the lunch period when it would cost appreciably less than during the dinner hours. If we wanted a light lunch, we munched hot dogs with kraut, huge pretzels, and Italian ices from the street vendors. We worked at avoiding the fast food chains. Frequently, we bought pizza slices and soft drinks, sweet rolls and sandwiches, coffee and candy at neighborhood delis and took them back to our room late afternoon or after a show.

Often after the theater is when we would have our most interesting meals, sometimes just at different <u>Howard Johnson's</u> where we would try exotic ice cream treats, but many times at a Bavarian restaurant called <u>Wienerwald</u>, where we loved the atmosphere, the friendliness (the hostess actually "remembered" us from year to year), the delicious dinners, the good wine, and their "Black Forest torte." That place is no more, and we miss it.

One of our special places was <u>Enrico and Pagliari's</u> in the basement of the Taft; it was an Italian restaurant with all-you-can-eat antipasto and all-you-can-drink Chianti or Sangria. We have also enjoyed lunches at the famous <u>Mama Leone's</u>, the <u>Hunan House</u> in Chinatown, and at many sidewalk or step-down cafes in "the Village." We have even had the privilege of dining in the <u>Delegates' Dining Room</u> at the United Nations.

NOTES FROM LATER:

- We once, early-on, walked blocks and blocks without finding a suitable breakfast place, and our mood deteriorated every extra step of the way; lesson learned; we want no bad moods in the city.

- We love those hotdogs with kraut from the carts especially up around Central Park or down in "the Village", lots of napkins for the juices running down our fingers; we have never worried about their safety, and we have never suffered from them.

- At a late lunch at Mama Leone's, a very popular and well-known place at the time, one we had wanted to visit, the waiter stood at our table, after we had paid the bill, with a stern look on his face and his hand extended until he was perfectly satisfied with our tip; he was not kidding either. And . . . neither am I.

- We once took the UN tour, and even had a chance to meet some of the delegates; when we were offered the opportunity to dine in the Delegates' Dining Room, we jumped at the chance; it was occasionally a possibility if the General Assembly was not in session, so that it was not too busy; we just lucked out, and we had a great lunch; it's a huge, bright, pleasant, multi-windowed area.

- September 21, 1987 -

The first Broadway show we saw was HAIR in its final week with Gerome Ragni (one of the writers and one of the original cast members) returning to play the lead again and to close out the production in style. The Sunday night that we were there . . . 3rd row center on the aisle . . . was his first night back. The energy, the excitement of the production and of the company added to our excitement; just being there was like an electric charge.

The way the show developed with actors just sort of wandering onto the stage, talking to the audience, just lazing about, and then slowly coming into focus, into action, was just mesmerizing. Other actors came down the aisles, some walking on the armrests of the seats among and beside us, and then . . . it happened and continued . . . the show was on; it really was a kind of "**happening**" *for the next two-plus hours.*

I danced in the aisle with a gorilla, clapped in time to the music, and ended up on stage after the show (as invited), moving in time to the music, and mingling with the cast. It was a wonderful initiation to Broadway. I got those great seats just a couple of hours before show time at their box office.

Other shows since then have been grander, have had better dancing, have had a stronger score, have had splashier sets, have featured bigger-name stars, have had a more serious book, have had finer costumes, more interesting lighting, and ever sharper sex, but . . . nothing ever equaled, for us, that first New York production; it was magic for all its allusion and illusion.

NOTES FROM LATER:

- HAIR was very much a product of "The Age of Aquarius" including the onstage nudity, which was our first encounter with such, but which we did not find offensive or crude, just a natural part of the show.

- A "happening" was sort of a hallmark of the age; it was an expanded, very intense experience, which is what everyone wanted in those days.

- We usually just went to the box offices of the shows we wanted to see only after we got to New York; we seldom failed to get good seats; only once were we separated in order to see the show at all; that was for EVITA; we did decide not to do that again; we like to feel the show together.

- Some of our other favorite shows (we especially love musicals) over the years: SWEENEY TODD (we never could get over the dynamics of that show from the "industrial revolution" styled set to the glint of light in all that darkness); BARNUM (I loved the circus theme, and we saw Jim Dale as Barnum and, soon-to-become-famous actor, Glenn Close as Charity Barnum; it is only one of two shows I have seen twice on Broadway); FOLLIES (our biggest heart-stopper was in the middle of this show when an actor forgot his lines . . . and . . . then . . . after what seemed like a very long pause . . . went on with the show . . . as it slowly dawned on us that it was all a part of the scene); PIPPIN (one of my favorite songs is from this show, "Corner of the Sky;" I am forever looking for my own little corner); and JESUS CHRIST SUPERSTAR (which enthralled us with its opening when the whole front curtain, or panel in this case, slowly lowered back to become the floor, and the actors climbed up and crawled over it into place; we also love this score, and have seen many other productions of that show).

- September 22, 1987 -

What is it about the people of New York that makes them so special? Is it that they know that they live in the most vital city in the country, if not the world? Is it the energy they absorb from one another? Is it the dynamism of the mix from the fact that once in New York, you become a New Yorker, which brings bits and pieces of Puerto Rico, Japan, Texas, Iowa, Italy, China, etc. and so forth, together to make something even greater, even more special, something more than just the sum of its parts.

I have found the people I've dealt with to be surprisingly warm and attentive if I can accept a certain brusqueness, a certain façade, which is necessary to withstand the brusqueness of life and the pressures of this power-packed city. A "please," a "thank-you," a smile, an extra moment's wait, a positiveness, an energy of one's own can help smooth the interpersonal relationships that are so much a part of this city. There are so many people who come to work here in the various capitals of industry, commerce, and the arts, and who come to visit for the shows, the sights, the restaurants, the time away; it's the ambience (the typical atmosphere or mood of a place) which is anything . . . and everything.

It is interesting to me that, at one time when I lived in this city of 8-10 million people, I felt terribly alone with no one, in particular, to talk to, and with no one to really care about me, until I took the time to make that kind of effort toward others. It was then we gelled and mixed and related and belonged . . . together.

NOTES FROM LATER:

- I love that multi-cultural mix; it is part of the vitality of the city. I have been all over Manhattan from Harlem to <u>Battery Park</u> (and most places in between); I have been from the west side, the <u>Jacob Javits Convention Center</u>, to the east side, the UN building. Everywhere I have been, I have met interesting people who were also, as it turned out, often interested in me, and who could easily be friends.

- The people who work in customer service are pretty matter-of-fact most of the time because they are at their jobs, but they are almost always knowledgeable, cooperative, friendly, and even fun. Only once have I been chased, literally, on leaving a restaurant where I had just eaten, because the waiter thought I had "stiffed" him; I hadn't; in fact, I had been overly generous, but he had not actually served us well, and he may have thought we would do just that. It's a true story.

- September 23, 1987 -

I know that regular New Yorkers have a love-hate relationship with the buildings that are the hallmark of their city. What one likes because it is gaudy or unique or classic or bold or clean, another just doesn't care for. I have some of my own personal favorites, for various reasons, and none that I really hate. Perhaps I'm not there enough to get that involved; perhaps I only see or remember the ones that make some kind of an impression on me.

Of course, I like the <u>Empire State Building</u>, what style, what élan as it points its way all the way up; I like <u>Lincoln Center</u> as a complex more than for each individual building; I have often rested on the concrete benches around the fountain in the center of the plaza. I like the <u>Pan-Am</u> building, a special monstrosity to many New Yorkers, because it sits astride another building and a street, and is not afraid to be what it is. I love the Gothic demeanor ("charm" is not quite the word) of the <u>Dakota</u> up on Central Park West; how I would love to get inside. I like the just-doesn't-quite-fit quality of the <u>Guggenheim Museum</u> with its spiraling ramps that speak to what it is. I love the aloofness (just enough, but not too much) of the <u>Frick Mansion</u>, now such a wonderful museum. I love the panache of the <u>Washington Square Arch</u> at the end of Fifth Avenue. I even like the twin towers of the <u>World Trade Center</u> (we've been to the top) despite their being taller than the <u>Empire State Building</u> which is still the granddaddy of them all. And . . . I love inside <u>Radio City Music Hall</u> which is the epitome of what a fine theater should be.

NOTES FROM LATER:

- Many years later, I had occasion to do business with a firm in the Empire State Building (even I'm impressed); that lends being there an entirely different élan than seeing it when one is just a tourist, but . . . as tourists, we have been to the top, to the observation deck several times. I remember the first time, I was quite taken with the idea that we had to take two different banks of elevators.

- I lived just a few blocks from the Dakota; I would often walk by there on my way home from work; it conjures images of the celebrities like John Lennon and Yoko Ono who lived there (and, of course, of that terrible tragedy); and it conjures other dark thoughts because of its brooding look, and its mere presence.

- I was just as stunned as everyone else when the 2 towers of the World Trade Center fell on 9/11. I was glad I had been there at one time, and sad that I could never go again, but even sadder that so many would never, nor could ever, come back from there.

- At Radio City Music Hall, there's that huge proscenium arch, that glorious organ, the stage that rises on an elevator, and revolves when needed to, and, of course, the "Rockettes". We've seen many stage shows there (some movies, as well), including the renowned Christmas show with its living nativity, live camels, sheep, and donkeys, and the snow falling all over inside the theater, and we've seen the "Rockettes" on tour all over the country.

- September 24, 1987 -

I think part of New York's glamour, if that's the word, is what it stands for as much as what it is. And . . . it stands for many things. With the <u>United Nations</u> located there on the East River, New York is really the center of international government, a rather impressive role for any city to play. There is a kind of special dynamic because of the delegations and their headquarters and their customs and their languages and their differences all actually living and working side by side by side. This is not to mention the high-powered visitors, heads of state, other dignitaries, who come and go, stopping traffic, turning heads, prompting demonstrations, and some very strong feelings.

New York is, of course, also the center of theater in America. Over the years it may have lost some of its shine to the burgeoning regional theaters (and maybe even to TV), but for all the magic there is in the word "abracadabra", there is even more in the collective noun, "Broadway."

Publishing, Finance, Fashion, Broadcasting, Art, and Advertising are some of the areas in which New York plays a pivotal role. It is almost more than a single city can live with and live up to. Yet, New York handles its varied roles pretty well under the circumstances, continuing to draw the very best, the very brightest, and the very toughest to its street and to its heart. It's a place where it's probably true that if you can succeed there, if you can survive there, baby, you can succeed and survive anywhere else. I have to admit, though, that I'm not quite sure what kind of success I had there, but . . . I surely gave it a good try.

NOTES FROM LATER:

- Since I wrote this section, the theater scene in NYC has bounced back, and it is currently thriving. As I write this, it is announced that this was the best season in history from all accounts. The whole area around the many theaters has been cleaned up, and, in too many cases sort of "Disneyfied"; there are several Disney-produced shows playing there now (great ones, too, like THE LION KING and MARY POPPINS); this is to say that it has been made more family-friendly; I must admit, sometimes, I think of it as being, just maybe, too pasteurized and too homogenized.

- Many of the older theaters, some which had been B-movie parlors for a long time, and some which were down and almost-out XXX porn palaces, have been renovated and updated, and are now legitimate and successful and quite beautiful mainstream theaters (where many of the Disney shows play).

- September 25, 1987 -

I think my favorite museum in Manhattan is the <u>Museum of the City of New York</u> up on 5th Avenue and 101st. It is not as large or as extensive or as pretentious or as busy as the <u>Metropolitan</u>, for instance, but one can spend hours there in comfort with some of the classiest exhibits in town; I remember seeing a fabulous exhibit that made good use of New York trash by making it truly look like art.

I think my favorite theater is the <u>New York State Theater</u> at <u>Lincoln Center</u>. I remember, once, on a tour of the complex, watching from the balcony a light-check for a single ballet dancer down on that stage. It was magic, all the imaginings I've ever had about the theater rolled into that moment.

I think my favorite street food is Italian ice. What I like is the refreshing quality on a warm summer day, and its availability; one doesn't have to seek it out as one does back home. The thing I don't like is the cost, naturally, and the fact that I never get enough at a time.

I think my favorite Broadway show was BARNUM; it is the only show I went to twice (except OH, CALCUTTA, but that was for entirely different reasons). I don't think others appreciate BARNUM like I do, but I would love to direct it. It is so theatrical, including the performances outside the theater before the actual show starts, and including the performers and musicians up and down the aisles giving it that true circus atmosphere.

NOTES FROM LATER:

- Sadly, we don't get up to 101st as often as we would like; it is so far uptown, and we have so many other things to do in our too-short stays, so we tend to keep to Midtown where so much else is always going on.

- I don't really have a favorite Broadway theater, but I have loved the <u>Winter Garden</u>, what was the <u>Mark Hellinger</u>, and the <u>Schubert</u>, and who doesn't love "Schubert Alley" (which runs through the heart of the show district) just before show times?

- One of my least favorite street foods is the chestnuts at holiday time; even though "roasting on an open fire" sounds so festive and so charming.

- I saw OH, CALCUTTA a second time to accompany someone who really wanted to see it; it is a beautiful show, but, you do know, perhaps, that it is quite about the nudity?

- I took my oldest son to New York as a graduation present from high school; he was the youngest in his class, but he graduated as the Valedictorian. I got tickets for what he especially wanted to see, a Stephen Sondheim show; we say SUNDAY IN THE PARK WITH GEORGE; he loved it; me . . . not so much.

- At one time, when I worked in NYC, I had seen every show then playing on the Broadway stage; I had seen some of the long-running ones the year or two before on business trips; I had seen more on a recent vacation; I had an unlimited "research" budget to see whatever else I wanted or needed to, and I definitely took advantage of that.

- September 26, 1987 -

Of course, New York can be bizarre. 42nd Street, alone, would qualify, with its string of marquees extolling violence and triple-X sex; with its porn shops and head shops, dirty diners, and other unsavory places; with its doorways reeking of urine, and often occupied by a drunk or two, and the indigent; with its trash and its litter and aromas; with its sidewalk shops of questionable and/or "hot" goods.

The people can be bizarre, too. I admit I had to stare at the young, bearded, long-haired fellow with no shirt, just an open vest over his many tattoos, and an inch-thick pipe through the pierce in his ear. I had to grin at the old "bag lady" who often parked on a bench near <u>Lincoln Center</u> and talked steadily and rapidly to herself; oh, I didn't grin at who she was or that she was doing all the talking, that's fairly familiar, but I grinned at her long, gray, thinning hair with its bits of paper, and string, and sticks, and other detritus woven into it, and how proud she was of it.

I had to be startled by the blatancy of the hookers (not recently, but a few years back before a conscious effort to clean things up); they were everywhere in the theater district, often in twos, often in the tallest plastic boots and the shortest mini-skirts, in the skimpiest of halter tops, the wildest of colored wigs, and always with a large handbag. They were not shy either, even if you were not alone; I was approached more than once. It was sad, really, that they were there at all, but especially in such numbers, and so young, and often black or some other minority.

I had to cringe at one old, poor, filthy fellow who talked to himself as he walked right out of his tattered, make-shift cardboard shoes; he shuffled or scurried from one garbage container to another, and he checked trash on the sidewalks, picking for food, munching/sucking on tossed chicken bones or on stale French fries,

> *and sipping or slurping from discarded soda cans or bottles or battered paper cups.*

NOTES FROM LATER:

- I soon became accustomed, almost immune, to such bizarreness; now we see it all around us wherever we are; it really has to be a special kind of shocker these days.

- I actually became familiar with that particular "bag lady;" I called her Amelia because that's what was on a sticker she had stuck on her jacket; she never denied it. We did chat briefly as I passed her bench each day on my way to work; it started with a "Good morning," and became a "How are you today?" and eventually "How nice you look;" in return she replied "Oh, my yes, it is, thank you;" "I feel so good, thank you;" and eventually "Thank you, I do don't I," as she stroked and fluffed her detritus-decorated hair.

- Years later the Times Square area and its surroundings was cleaned up, and the hookers were all gone, or, at least, not visible anymore; Midtown has been gentrified, and, as I've said before, pasteurized and homogenized; I call it "Disneyfied."

- I've seen too many people eating from the trash and from the street; drinking from discarded cans and bottles; picking up cigarette butts and making them into a fine satisfaction; it is all too sad any place at all, but here, as sad as it is, it is just a part of the scene.

- September 27, 1987 -

And there are other bizarre things to an outsider. I think the sidewalk vendors are bizarre; the large displays of sunglasses on blankets or cardboards, for instance; the umbrellas that appear for sale, like magic, as rain threatens; the fireworks right out of inside coat pockets. 3-card Monte is bizarre; who would believe that anyone could still be suckered by that old scam? Are we that desperate to win a buck? Or . . . are we that eager to lose one?

I think the prices charged for show tickets are bizarre; Prices, in general, have to be considered pretty weird: a barely adequate apartment for a thousand bucks or more; lunch for a mere $50.00 a person; tolls to even get in or out of the city. And what about the food? Does anyone really like or even dare to eat sushi from the street? Or falafel? How do we know that the hotdogs and kraut are anywhere near being safely edible? It's certainly not from the vendor's appearance. Want some candy or nuts or cheese or fruit from right next to the sewer vents, the street dust and dirt, the urine splashes and smells, the spittle, and . . . God knows what else?

The subway is also bizarre: the graffiti all over the cars, the filth on the floors, the dark and depressing lighting in the stations, the noise, the cram of riders, the "hangers-out" everywhere one turns.

Do you know what else is really bizarre? It's bizarre that we can accept it all as just a part of this very vital city where, essentially, everyone is welcome. It's like a test that makes us stronger and better for taking it and for passing.

NOTES FROM LATER:

- Remember, these short essays were written in 1987; times have changed, prices have changed (show tickets are now in the hundreds), attitudes have changed (not always for the better), and so have I; I get it now, even if I don't necessarily want it.

- Of course, we indulged in street food; I love the hotdogs and kraut from those sidewalk carts especially when we're up near the Park, and I kept one of those miniature Coke bottles as a souvenir for a long time.

- September 28, 1987 -

One of my favorite things about the city is its walkability. I have taken a cab; I have ridden the subway; I have been on a bus; I have been in a van and a car; I have cruised on a boat, and shuttled on a ferry. I have, even, taken a carriage ride through <u>Central Park</u>, but, mostly, during my many visits and during the time I lived there, I have walked.

Once my wife and I walked all the way down Fifth Avenue from Midtown to the Village through a wonder of different neighborhoods and cultural districts. We have walked from the Village back up Broadway to the theater district; some places along the way are like war zones, other areas like shopping malls; the mix also includes parks and good living space. We have walked from the <u>United Nations</u> building across town to and through <u>Central Park</u>. We have walked on a museum excursion from 101st, the <u>Museum of the City of New York</u>, down to 89th to the <u>Guggenheim</u>, on to 82nd, the <u>Metropolitan</u>, and, then, to 70th to the <u>Frick</u> and, finally, on to the <u>American Craft Museum</u> at 53rd.

We have walked all around Chinatown, Little Italy, Soho (that's <u>SO</u>uth of <u>HO</u>uston), Greenwich Village, and Lower Manhattan and Wall Street. Most of all, we have walked Midtown to the theaters to get tickets and back for the shows; to the stores to buy clothes and souvenirs; to the tourist attractions (I think we've seen them all); to gawk at the skyscrapers and to gawk at the people; to go find interesting and inexpensive places to eat.

When I lived there, I walked from pretty far uptown to work each day, and then back home again; I lived at the <u>Esplanade</u> on West End Avenue at 74th. I loved the crowds of walkers, and I loved being one of their number. How civilized to have such a walkable city, and from my point of view, at least, such a safe one with taking

> *into account one's own particular care, discretion, awareness, and concern.*

NOTES FROM LATER:

- I would say that, for the most part, we never felt uncomfortable, certainly not afraid, we just felt tired and foot-sore. We once saw a thief grab and run with a tourist's camera, but we never witnessed a mugging.

- We never walked late at night or in dangerous places; we stayed where the people were. Once, after a show, we did walk across town on 57th from Lincoln Center to our hotel; we could have caught a pedicab or a taxi, but we wanted to walk; we weren't afraid; we weren't nervous; our only problem was some difficulty in finding a good place to have a drink and a late-night snack.

- One of our more recent discoveries is Chelsea; we love it, all the small shops, the unique little cafes/bistros, the quaintness of the buildings, the small theaters, and, again, the walkability. We both agree, all things being equal, we could move there.

- September 29, 1987 -

New York is, I suppose, a city in which anything can happen, and, some would say, usually does. It should come as no surprise, then, that certain incidents occurred that definitely seemed out of the ordinary. I was rushing to the <u>Palace Theater</u> to get tickets for WOMAN OF THE YEAR; just as I got to the corner, the light changed, so being the good Midwesterner I am, I waited to cross (unlike most others); as I waited I looked around at the traffic and the crowds gathered by the <u>TKTS</u> booth (half price show tickets); when I turned, I recognized some long-time friends from back home who were there on vacation; we were all quite stunned, and, then, we were all quite delighted.

I landed a job in New York in one day. I went to <u>Eaves Costume</u> for a visit and for a tour; I was asked, before I left there, to consider a serious job offer, and to come back the next day with my decision. It seemed too good to be true, too good to refuse, so I took it! It was too good to be true, as it turned out . . . for a variety of reasons . . . but . . . just think of that!

I remember about a hometown girl on a school field trip who left or lost her billfold in a taxi or a bus, and had it arrive back at her home by mail before she and the tour group got back.

We were walking up Central Park West one day and discovered a large <u>Lutheran</u> church named <u>Holy Trinity</u>, the same name and synod as our church back home. We call that serendipity. We went there several times after that on our annual visits to Manhattan; they had a professional quartet singing each Sunday in the summer. One Sunday morning we went early enough to stop for brunch at the famous <u>Mayflower Hotel</u>; it is just across from the Park; it is one of our favorite memories.

NOTES FROM LATER:

- The friends I ran into asked for suggestions for a show that a family could enjoy; I suggested BARNUM; they saw it and enjoyed it just as I had twice before.

- At one point, during WOMAN OF THE YEAR (which starred Lauren Bacall), the set stalled moving in from stage right; Lauren was riding on the hood of a car, as if in a parade; it just did not want to move forward, so . . . she called out to the crew "Let's take it back and start over again." We applauded as they did just that, and after a moment the set glided smoothly into place; we applauded again; Lauren waved, took a bow, and the scene went on.

- Since I was considered the most successful costumer-from-stock in the country, I was hired to bring <u>Eaves</u> and recently purchased <u>Brooks Van Horn</u> (another large costumer) together; it was a tough and tricky job, but, then, it was New York, and somebody had to do it. That somebody was me!

- September 30, 1987 -

When I began to write about New York, and how I feel about it, I thought I might have something new to say. Now, I'm not so sure that I do. Lots of people have a love affair with this city; lots of people have a hate affair, too. I just know that, once there, I felt a kinship, as if we were really in sync. I continue to feel that way even though, at one time, I left the city abruptly, because I just couldn't live with it. I find that I can take the city more on my terms than on its.

I do believe that I appreciate the city more as a friend who visits rather than as a live-in-lover. I like being able to take the city on my own terms rather than being forced to accept it on its own terms. I miss it when I'm not there; I yearn to return; I ponder it; I read about it; I dream of being there. I get an enormous jolt at planning a visit, at setting dates, at making reservations, at anticipating. I get some kind of a "high," albeit a strangely mellow one on landing there, on traveling into Midtown, on experiencing, one more time, the bustle, the people, the traffic, the buildings, the smells, the lights, the sights, the city!

I get a thrill at being a New Yorker for another little while, for doing New York things another time. I never get tired of it. But . . . at some time, I am ready to go home, so that I can, some other time, turn around, come back, and savor it all again.

NOTES FROM LATER:

- Usually we planned our own trips, but, one year, we scheduled our trip with AAA; we were so busy, and just needed someone else to tend to the details. It was at Thanksgiving time, so we got to actually be at Macy's "Thanksgiving Day Parade", and we had a posh dinner in Bryant Park (behind the Library) in a tent with carpet, with draperies, with fine linen, with silver service, with fine wines and . . . with delicious, traditional Thanksgiving food.

- When we were deciding where to go on a special trip for our 50th wedding anniversary, we agreed instantly that we wanted to go back to New York one more time, and we had a fabulous time doing the things we had done many times before, and, of course, trying out a few new ones. We happened upon a short stretch of West 46th Street nicknamed "Restaurant Row;" there were dozens of small cafes, quaint bistros, fancy restaurants, and lots of delicious aromas, intriguing signs, and eager hosts and hostesses to invite us in. We were especially taken with it, because, back home, we live on what is designated "Eat Street," with much the same array of good places to eat. Of course, we dined there! We selected "Don't Tell Mama" because of its quaint name, its piano cabaret, its lovely step-down garden, and, as it turned out, its fine Italian food.

– CHAPTER FIFTEEN –

Hi, Tubby! Hey, Slim!

I was a fat kid; there's no getting around it; there's no hedging; I was a fat kid. I was always the fattest, sometimes the biggest, probably the softest kid in my grade and in the grades around mine. I was called all the unpleasant and hurtful epithets when I was in grade school and junior high: "Fatso," "Fatty," "Tubby," "Tub-a-lard," "Porky." I sort of got used to it, tried to take it like a man, and made up for it by my successes in all other things except physical activity. I kept myself clean, and I dressed reasonably well. I didn't lack friends, but, sometimes, the so-called *cool* kids just taunted me, or, mostly, just left me alone.

When I got into high school, things changed quite a bit; over the years I had earned some respect for being a *straight-A* student, as an "expert" in a variety of things, as a good citizen, and for my singing and acting and public speaking talents. It is also true that, every once in awhile, when I really needed to, I could handle any threat to who I was; you can ask about so and so . . . no names, please . . . and what was a big surprise to many when I chased him after he teased me, grabbed him, threw him to the ground, sat on him, and beat the heck out of him.

I had many friends who knew me for what I was worth, and not just how I looked; anyway, I wasn't ugly, actually pretty normal-looking except for my size; I was just big. It was out of that respect, then, that I came to be known as "Big Bud," a name which stuck with me for many years. In fact, in the 1955 yearbook, the class "will" (a project for the seniors) says, "Leroy Prescott leaves PHS . . . without a 'Big Bud'."

All that being said, I always dreamed of being slim and trim. I got there after I left home and went away to college. I dropped 30 pounds over that summer and into the fall. I was working at the <u>Minneapolis Star and Tribune</u>, and eating less, and doing lots of walking just to get around. I wasn't having home-cooked meals which had certainly contributed to my generous size. My mother was a good cook, and . . . my dad was a trained chef, and we owned a restaurant. We ate well. I seldom, if ever, remember going without a meal, let alone ever being hungry.

My dad had opened his first restaurant right after graduating from high school; his mother had signed for him to be able to do it; he learned a lot about good cooking and good food from her; she was a great cook; she encouraged people to eat; she was sort of *zaftig* herself. Eventually my dad went to cooking school, and when he was drafted, he was the chief chef of his Navy unit, the "Seabees".

My mother had learned to cook at the side of her mother and older sister; she never cared much for it, though. As a teenager, she had other things on her mind; she wanted to be more of a socialite; she lived in the country, but would be moving to town for high school. She met my dad as a Freshman in high school; he was a popular Senior; she could not believe that he was actually interested in her, but she was very attractive, really quite aware, and a pretty good catch herself. They married right after she graduated, and she had to come to like cooking, since she worked side by side with him for 35 years in the café business. She had to learn his secrets, and to prepare things to his specifications (and he was demanding), so . . . the food was very good, and we always ate well.

When on my own, I ate a light breakfast, never one of my favorite meals (so I usually skipped it growing up), but provided at my first job. I ate a good lunch daily at one of the city's best cafeterias, <u>The Forum</u>; I loved their tomato and celery salad (notice no lettuce), and their Salisbury steak. I could only afford so much, so I ate less than I would usually have. For supper, I often ate in my room, usually it consisted of a pint of <u>Dairy Queen</u>, half a bag of potato chips, and some soda; I preferred root beer.

I continued to lose throughout my Freshman year in college; I was too busy, too often, to worry about eating, and I was too busy, too often, just walking from here to there and back again day after day; I was also working part-time, taking a full load of classes (on a big campus), and I had no car; sometimes I didn't have all that much extra cash for bus fare or snacks either.

I never regained the weight that I lost (until I was much older), and I am glad to say that I do not weigh today even close to what I weighed when I graduated from high school. Did I mention that I, then, weighed 244 pounds?

The lowest I weighed as an adult was 151 pounds the summer I got married; that's 93 pounds less than at one time. I was, 6 feet tall, so at that point, I was rather gaunt, as a matter of fact, but I had always wanted to be slim and trim, and I had, finally, truly made it.

Married life added some pounds; my wife is another excellent cook; she is, especially, an excellent baker (woe is me), but I maintained my efforts to stay in good shape through many years being busy as a husband, then as a father (of 1 . . . 2 . . . 3 sons), then as a home owner, and all that time as an intense, dedicated teacher, director, mentor, and union organizer. I liked my new look; actually, I liked the whole new me.

I had the capacity, over the years, to take control if I gained a bit, and I needed to lose again. My women friends, especially, used to just hate the fact that if I said I needed to lose ten pounds, I would set a period of time, adjust my food intake, increase my activity, and . . . just do it. Oh, yes, indeed, they used to hate that.

I still keep an eye on my weight; I weigh everyday, and I actually mark it down in my journal; then, if I escalate a bit, I can catch it right away, and just cut down on my food intake. But, let's face it, even if I don't eat any more than I ever did, it's not as easy as it used to be to keep it off. Oh, to be slim and trim again, fit and healthy and fine . . . forever.

– CHAPTER SIXTEEN –

I Shoulda' Coulda' Been

There is a line in the movie, ON THE WATERFRONT, where the washed-up prizefighter (a "pug," really) bemoans to his older brother that he coulda' been a contenda'. The actor playing that part was Marlon Brando, at his best, with Karl Malden, at his best, as the brother. I used this film in high school media classes to talk about serious movies, dramas, if you will; I watched it more than once a day in more than one class for more than one high school quarter, year after year; I never got tired of it, but, when I think back on it, I realize that I probably never coulda' been a contenda'.

I was not a very good athlete . . . ever. My claim to fame is that I once served seventeen times in a row to win a volley ball tournament and to surprise the heck out of everyone else involved. I have a ribbon to prove it, with my name on it and everything.

I was a big, fat kid; I wasn't in any kind of shape or condition to be a sports figure unless it was a Sumo wrestler. I wasn't fast enough to win a race (unless I was running away from a couple of bothersome bullies who were never able to catch me because I was way smarter than they were); I couldn't do a pull-up or much of a pushup to save my soul, and what the heck is a burpee? If I hit the ball, it could go far, but I had a poor swing, often over, under, around, or through; if I had to run the bases . . . "You're out!"

I did play varsity football for one year in high school; it was my dad's idea; he had played most sports years before at the same high school. I was a right tackle; I was in that front line, just planted there, because I was so big and so solid that few could get around or by me; I was brave enough, and not at all afraid to take a hit with all that padded gear on. I was smart enough to remember what I was supposed to do, and often clever enough to outwit or surprise the opponents by making some least expected move to mess up their plays. I did earn my team letter; it's in a drawer somewhere.

I tried out for basketball, because I loved it and played it as often as I could, but I wasn't tall enough and, certainly, not fast enough to ever make a varsity team. The thing was that I was . . . a terrific shot; I had a great eye. I had practiced for hours at the basket on our garage; I could hit 100 free throws in a row, again and again, no problem; I could beat any of the neighbor kids or relatives, or even many of the local athletes. We played lots of pickup games. Eventually, we had regulation-height standards and baskets installed on our adjacent vacant lot with precise markings on the clay court. I never got enough of the game; when the state tournaments were on TV (or even in just the radio days) I watched and listened in earnest. For years, I went to every game our hometown team played at home or away, and I kept score, field goals, free throws, and percentages (in a pocket notebook that went everywhere with me); at different times, I even got to work the statistics at real games.

I bought my first TV set (17 inches, black and white, on a metal stand) in the spring after we were married, so that we could watch the state high school basketball tournaments. When I was older, and had cable TV, and had some time off, I watched 37 games (all levels of playing) in 10 days.

I was the ball boy for my dad's "kitten ball" team, and I kept their statistics, too; this was in a town league; our team was one of the best, as I remember it; we even recruited some "ringers" from the farming areas around. If I understand it, "kitten ball" is a precursor name for softball, so-called because the originator team was called the "Kittens," and it actually started indoors as a winter version of baseball and with a softer ball.

I had aspirations; I had the desire; I loved the connections; I had the dreams of being a part of a team, any old team; I wallowed in the history, and the development, and the records, and the attention from the public. I still relish all of the above.

But . . . this is sort of a sad dream; It just wasn't what I was cut out for. I tried, but I never really succeeded; I'm not sorry about it; I'm quite resigned; I am who and how and what I am. I remain a fan. I love to see my grandkids play soccer, or football, or just shooting baskets. I've discovered rugby since my oldest grandson played and was the most valuable player on a state-championship team (and I've also witnessed the breaking of his nose).

I've seen the Twins play many times at all their venues; we were in the stands at the old <u>Metropolitan Stadium</u> when Harmon Killebrew hit his 500th and 501st homeruns (my son now has those ticket stubs); I've been to <u>World Series</u> games; I have my collection of "Homer Hankies." On my 60th birthday, the scoreboard lit up between innings (as arranged by my sons) with "Happy 60th Birthday to Bud Prescott." That's another kind of thrill.

– CHAPTER SEVENTEEN –

Who Else Would I Be?

I have more often dreamed of being a certain kind of person rather than being any specific one, but there are those whom I've admired enough (even idolized), whom I've been envious of (sort of sad, I guess), or have just plain liked.

Let's see. Where do I start? With whom? What is the first name that comes to mind?

That first is Johnny Carson; I would have liked to be who and what and how he was, at least as far as his public image. I would have loved to be a star on TV as a talk show host; I would have loved his quick wit and comic timing; I would have loved to be so suave; and I would still love to be so admired. We once stood in line to see his show in Las Vegas, but it was sold out, and our dreams of getting in were dim unless, perhaps, we could pony up a couple more large bills (that's "hundreds"). We did, though, see him when he cut through the line just in front of us as he and his entourage made their way into the showroom. No, don't be silly, grown men don't swoon; what's one skipped beat of the heart? I would not have wanted his detachment, his aloofness, his need for security, his different divorces, his estrangement from his sons. Let me pick the best parts of who he was, since this is just one of my dreams.

I think I would like to be John Grisham, the popular and successful novelist of legal matters, crime, and social consciousness. I've read all his adult novels; I look forward to the next one's release. He also has a series of young people's detective stories. I don't think that everything he writes is great, that they are even, necessarily, good literature (some are better than others), but they all are darn good reads; I devour them as do millions of others.

If someone is talented, successful, popular, and just plain nice, then, that's who I might want to be, that's whom I would emulate, that's whom I admire the most. I would want to be known and remembered that way. We probably don't even know much about the best of those people, the people who are all the above, but who stay out of the limelight, the ones who make a difference behind the scenes with no publicity necessary.

I might as well take the time to name a few others whom I admire, whom I would choose to be, if such were possible. You may not like all of my list, and that's as it should be; it's *my* list; you might just have some such list of your own; think about it.

The first President I ever voted for was John F. Kennedy; I loved the "Camelot" years; they ended too tragically and much too soon. Who knows what might have been? Oh, sure, there's always "dirt" to be dug up; there are always things to be buried; with the current "open market" about virtually everybody, that's a part of reality, not the stuff of dreams.

I never saw Helen Hayes on stage, but she is the epitome' of a great actor (I prefer to use that designation; whoever heard of a doctress or a lawyess or a teachess?). I have read much about her, have seen interviews with her, and have seen her on film. She was the *grande dame* of theater who, forever, nonetheless, embodied the ingénue. Did you know that for all those years on Broadway, and through all those successes, she was seriously allergic to the dust backstage, but . . . she was the personification of the concept that the show must go on.

I am a huge fan of Leonard Bernstein. I think his capacities to conduct classical music, to teach children, and to write musical comedy scores are remarkable. One of my favorite scores is from

CANDIDE (a story that I first encountered as a humanity text in college, and which was one of my favorites then). I once skipped part of my birthday party with my family to see and hear a concert version of the show. This musical has always been considered problematic to and for directors and producers and actors, too, but its OVERTURE is so beautiful and so provocative, and so precise, that it has become its own well-deserved "classic." And while we're at it, how beautiful is "Make Our Gardens Grow," another tune from that same show?

Okay, I know I'll be in trouble here with some of my readers, and I realize that I am giving away more of my political bent than I usually do, but . . . I am a true admirer of Bill Clinton and Hillary Rodham Clinton. I know that they both are problematic, and that they both have a "past," but then I say, "Who doesn't?" "He that is without sin among you, let him first cast a stone . . ." (that's in the BIBLE). They also, have another dimension, the other kind of past, one of hard work, of intelligence, of decisiveness, of social consciousness, of a willingness to serve, of an honest concern, and of truly caring. Past, present, future, we knew them once, we know them now, and who knows whether we will know them ongoing?

And, then, there is Jimmy Carter. Who wouldn't want to be that man? As I finish this chapter, he is much in the news for his diagnosis of terminal cancer; He has taken the news with such grace, and he intends to just keep on keeping on; he is 90 years old. He is a true humanitarian, and a relentless contributor of himself to the right causes; and, there is, of course, that <u>Nobel Peace Prize</u>.

Several years ago, after he was President, I heard him speak at a conference in San Antonio (one of my favorite cities, by the way); he was magnificent. I always said that if he had presented himself as well when he was President, if he had always spoken as eloquently, as clearly, and as precisely, he would have been President again (except, of course, for political machinations and, just maybe, the <u>Trilateral Commission</u>). I had a chance to meet him after the speech; he was so affable, so genuine, so real; it was like he was in a room full of old friends, and he appreciated seeing every one of them again. Who wouldn't want to be that man? I certainly would.

– CHAPTER EIGHTEEN –

The Real Me, By the Numbers

I count things. I record things. I list things. I balance my checkbook regularly, whether it needs it or not. This is just another part of the reality side of me, that is to say, it is not the dreamer at work nor the dreaming side. Here we have an assortment of miscellaneous, but very real, and, maybe even, rather important, stuff about this old man. There's no place to start really. I like to just jump right in to the middle of the things (*in medias res*). Let's see what might be sort of interesting.

I've owned 15 cars starting with a 1955 blue and white Buick Riviera hardtop convertible that my dad helped me buy at Stephens Buick in Minneapolis; he was always a Buick man; the first of his cars I remember was a 1939 Buick Special. I drove my Buick until I married Arlis; she had a 1956 black and gray Oldsmobile 88 that she had purchased second or third-hand from her uncle; we kept the newer one.

I've had 28 jobs starting with regular work for my dad in his restaurant business (I've washed more dishes, swept more floors, checked more coats, and stocked more counters and coolers than you can even imagine).

The first outside job I had was supplying worms for my Uncle's gas station bait box; I earned $1.20 for the first batch, 10 cents a dozen; I, actually, still have that dollar bill; I squandered the 20 cents on candy and soda.

I started my last job when I was 70 working as a Security Guard at the <u>Minneapolis Institute of Arts</u> (now <u>Art</u>), a major museum; I did that job for 7 years until I finally retired due to health reasons.

My career job was, of course, 21 years of teaching in public high schools (Sheldon, IA, New Prague, MN, Olivia, MN, and the <u>East Central Consortium</u>); for several of those years I was, also, <u>Language Arts Department</u> chairperson, and, of course, I supervised years of assorted extra-curricular activities.

We've lived in 15 different homes; that doesn't count our growing-up years (add 3 here for me, and just 1 for Arlis), or our college years (rooms and dorms and frat houses, 6 for me and just 1 for Arlis); not always memorable, nor the stuff that dreams are made of, but roofs over our heads.

The first house we ever owned together was a two-story, three-bedroom, Mediterranean-style with a full basement, an attached garage, and a flat roof; there were tall arborvitae on either side of the front door, and a huge yard in back for the kids to play in; it was the Mayor's house that had to be sold as part of an estate; we were thrilled to get it. It was on a one-way street, and was just one block north of the main street, just four blocks to school, and three blocks from church.

The house we lived in the longest was my boyhood home, which we bought from my mother after my dad died; she continued to live part of the year with us; our sons grew up there; we made many improvements over the years especially in finishing the basement; my favorite addition was the full-front screen porch.

We now live in a condo in the heart of the city, which we bought when it was, literally, still a hole in the ground, and which we helped to design and grow, and which we continue to love.

The Real Me, By the Numbers

I have lived in 12 different towns or cities from Princeton, MN where I was born, to other middle-American places, where I taught, to New York City to Margate and Coral Springs in south Florida, which was a surprise to us in that we were surprised to be there, and surprised that we really liked it.

I've had 13 pets through the years; I actually purchased my first puppy, whom I called Curly because of his tail, for fifty cents at the Mille Lacs County Fair; we've had parakeets, dogs, turtles, rabbits, and cats or kittens; our last pet was a tabby named Hobbes whom we rescued from a boy named Storm whose mother realized what a relief that would be for all concerned.

I have seen (and have the Playbills to prove it) 75 Broadway shows actually on what is the *real* "Broadway;" I have seen dozens of other professional productions from coast to coast, and, literally, hundreds of amateur productions. We also, regularly, attended the Metropolitan Opera when it toured. Who can ever forget that five-hour AIDA?

I've directed 29 plays or musicals in high schools, community theaters and summer stock; I've already mentioned THE MIRACLE WORKER as a highlight; but I need, also, to mention my adaptation of ROMEO AND JULIET (to make it more accessible to students and to provide more parts for women; it has subsequently been presented by other school groups); there was THE MUSIC MAN (which was the kickoff to a community's Bicentennial celebration, and which was plagued, one night, by a bomb scare); Arlis played the Mayor's wife, Eulalie MacKecknie Shinn. I'm very proud of SPOON RIVER ANTHOLOGY (poems about life and death selected from one of my favorite anthologies and supplemented with folk music) which was nothing short of professional, and where two non-performers found their niche and stole the show; and, then there was ANTIGONE (which I have always thought of as my "protest" production and which got me into the papers as a "played-out teacher" when I tried to resign from that enforced part of my job just to prove a point; those were the "union" years.

I've helped in dozens of other productions, as well, in almost all other stage capacities such as lighting (I'm really pretty good at that; I love the follow-spot); choreography (I really tried hard, maybe too hard, because I fell and broke my ankle and had to talk it through); flying (pulling the taut piano wire for Michael in a college-production of PETER PAN); costumes (with my wife who is a *wiz* with a sewing machine especially when she's using my designs); makeup (this is a particular strength, and lots of fun); and set construction (this is probably a weakness of mine . . . no . . . not probably . . . it *really* is).

Since high school, I've appeared in 15 plays or musicals; my favorite parts were Alfred P. Doolittle (Alfie) in MY FAIR LADY (with two buddies where we were called "a triumph" as a dancing trio after having learned it all new together), and Vernon T. Hines (Hinesie) in THE PAJAMA GAME (opposite my wife as Mable where we had one terrific duet about who could trust whom, and where I had to drop my pants on cue to prove a point).

I collect mugs; I have about 300; it started with the ones one gets as souvenirs when traveling, but, then, it became sort of an obsession; other travelers started bringing me souvenirs; I've bought some at flea markets and second-hand stores; I have beer mugs and steins, and shaving mugs and mustache cups from other eras. Once my two oldest sons were on a trip with a school group, and they each bought me a present; when they got back home, although they had shopped separately, they discovered that they had each gotten me the exact same mug; coincidentally, for their mother, who collects teaspoons, they had each gotten her the exact same spoon. Arlis collects lots of things, too, but her best collection is some fine bone china teacups and saucers, especially from England and Germany, which she hauls out when she wants us to feel just a *touch* elegant.

Are these all real numbers, or are they here just for effect? They are, trust me, very real numbers indeed. I may not have made it quite clear yet, but, I am a list-maker; I always have been; I make lists to help me get started, and to help me make progress, and to help me get through, and . . . I make lists to help me remember (that gets harder every day), and to help others know something about who I really am (if, in fact, they care).

I have these lists on file (oh, yes, we have files for most everything, as well), with my journals. I started journaling in 1987 on the occasion of my 50th birthday, and I have not missed a day since; (that's over 10,000 pages to this date, and each page has a title). The journals are all written in pencil (so that I can erase if necessary; I *do* make mistakes way too often) on narrow-lined (so-called "college-ruled") notebook paper. After a year's worth, I take them from their notebooks and store them in manila folders. We don't refer to them often, but, every once in awhile, they answer a question, prompt a memory, or settle an argument. I don't know what will eventually happen to them, but I will keep doing them as long as I can, and, then, they will be someone else's consideration, as my wife says "to enjoy, or . . . to destroy.".

As I am finishing this manuscript, I have switched to doing my daily journal pages on the computer; that was a hard decision to make; I am so much a creature of habit, but . . . I have some after-effects from my strokes so that even I can no longer read my handwriting.

– CHAPTER NINETEEN –

To Sleep, Perchance to Dream

And, then, there are the real dreams; I mean the ones I have when I am truly asleep, and which I have no control over, one way or another; maybe, the same sort of dreaming you do. I do dream regularly; sometimes (actually quite often) in full color; sometimes, there are just spots of strong color sort of punctuating the black and white or gray.

I remember lots of my dreams. I have even tried to train myself to remember more of them than most people can. I have been able to do that by relaxing, first of all, then not concentrating, keeping as clear and open a mind as possible, and . . . just trying to forget them. If you think that sounds odd, it probably is, but, it has worked, more than once. And when it does, it is so less frustrating than not being able to remember at all what a great or interesting experience you just woke up from.

The ones I am including here are the recurring ones, the ones that suggest to me some of my serious and varied interests, and, just maybe, some certain things that I still do not consider finished.

There are several dreams related to my connection to the theater. This is the most often reoccurring one: I am an actor who has not learned his lines by opening night, and who is cramming hard to remember them all, or who is just planning to go on anyway, just forge ahead, and fake it; I am terribly nervous and concerned about this failure to get done what I know I should have done by this very time. Let it be said, I am not a fast study; I have to read and reread the lines; I have to copy them over and over again;

as I study them, I have to be prompted and prompted once, twice, etc. and so forth; but . . . I have always made it on time.

This is another: I am playing Alfie Doolittle in a production of MY FAIR LADY (which I actually did in an awful community theater production where Alfie and his cronies were the very best part); I am late; the musical is already progressing toward my entrance; I am not even in costume yet, and it takes time to get dressed, as it is, but . . . I can't even find or get into the dressing area, which seems to be high up from the stage, or in a very back room. Of course, I am trying to do lines as I am getting ready, and . . . I definitely need a little bit of Alfred P. Doolittle's kind of luck.

Sometimes the set is not done; the audience is already filing in; the front curtains, for some reason are still open; we are trying to make it look as if the activity on the stage, and the open or bare spots, are just a part of the show. In reality, on one show, we actually were still painting the set and setting the doors, and hanging the drapes as the audience arrived, but they never knew that, because when the curtains opened, we were in our places and ready for the show to go on.

Sometimes, I can't get the very messy backstage areas cleaned up and in the order they need to be for the show to run well, or in the order they need to be when the show is over, and the borrowed or rented venue must be as it was when we loaded in; no one will help; often, I am the only one there; I never know if I get it done.

Another frequent dream: I am in a large foreign city (or maybe even New York), perhaps London, maybe Paris, and I am lost; I've taken off by myself or with a random companion to explore the wonders of the fascinating place, wherever it is; now, I can't find my way to any of the landmarks I want to see, or I can't find my way back to where I need to be to reconnect with the tour group, and, every once in awhile, I end up at an X-rated movie house on some obscure skid row; excuse me! I never do get back to my group, and I never do get to see the XXX movies either.

Sometimes, I am rushing to get to the plane which will take our tour group home again; the area leading to the boarding gate or ticket booth is always a long, wide, descending concrete ramp; I sometimes make it on time, but, most times, I am left behind. If I make it, the plane (which can be just as often a bus) is overcrowded, and uncomfortable and really awful.

Other times, I have run out of money, wherever I am, and, although the tour is with a large group of my friends (although none of them is recognizable, each of them is vaguely familiar), no one will help me; they all think I can afford this trip, this place, better than any of them can. I am waiting for money to be wired to me, as if I had some wealthy patron waiting in the wings; I never get home.

Lately, I have been dreaming more and more often about people whom I remember and miss. I seldom, if ever, dream about strangers or icons or personalities or celebrities or anyone historical. No, rather, I dream about seeing someone familiar, some loved one, some one from my past; I dream of meeting up with them again. Perhaps, I am thinking about my current time of life, and my getting closer to actually meeting them again. I hope that when I do, it's in a nice, high, airy, comfortable place, and not one that is way too deep, way too dark, and way to warm.

I dream, fairly often, about my mother; she was ill for the last years of her life; she had had a heart valve replacement, but she had survived that for another ten years; she died at 89. My sister was her preeminent caregiver, but we shared that responsibility on regular occasions. Myrtle was actually more a part of my life in these later years than she had been since I first moved away from home; she was with us every other or every third weekend. She loved to eat, and we fixed special dishes for her, not new things, but many of her old favorites: goulash, sauerkraut, molasses cookies, meatloaf; she loved to go out for a hamburger or some tasty soup.

She loved to play games, especially card games and games with dice; we played a game called "10,000" that she especially liked. She was an intense competitor; we accused her of having a tricky, arthritic, little finger that helped her flick those dice just the way she wanted them to land. As with most of the people in my dreams, she is somewhat evasive until she realizes who I am, and, then, she doesn't actually welcome me, but merely accepts me and adjusts to my being there . . . wherever *there* is.

Interestingly, I don't recall ever dreaming about my dad. He died fairly young, in 1971, of a long, debilitating illness; he was just 57. I have no particular explanation of why that would be; I remember him; he was a big presence in my life early on. But, then . . . he was just gone.

I also find it rather interesting that I do not dream about my wife or my sons and their families. I guess that they are all my dreams come true, and they are not just dreams to me; they are oh-so-real, and they mean oh-so-much to me. That is my reality; it just makes dreams suffer by comparison.

I dream about meeting old friends again; I think of that as some fun. I like that kind of meeting in real life, too. I especially enjoy encountering a former associate from my working years, who was so charming and really quite witty and something of a mentor to me; he is always smaller than I remember him (he was not very tall in the first place). He is just as delighted to see me again, as I am to see him. We had lunch together (sometimes, in those days, with two martinis) Friday after Friday for years when we worked together. He and his family and our family had some great times together over many years; we annually decorated a Christmas tree on their deck just for the birds; we used ornaments made from appropriate food; those are times that we cherish, and which we will never forget.

I seldom dream evil, scary, even very sad things; I don't have nightmares except for those that are filled with mental and emotional trauma (certainly not monsters), and I am never in fear for my life; it seems that I am just in fear of life itself. I remember, as a grade-schooler, seeing a movie with Abbott and Costello, a famous movie comedy team, meeting Frankenstein's monster; I had a real nightmare that night, such a very scary dream, that I woke up everybody else in the house with my screaming and crying. I remembered that film for a long, long time; I had flashes of some scenes even when I was awake; I can still recall the menace mixed in with what was supposed to be the fun of that film. I think I just might like to see it again, now . . . or . . . maybe . . . not!

I do like scary movies, though, and scary books; have you ever read THE EXORCIST or ROSEMARY'S BABY? Have you ever seen the movies? Now, there are a couple of nightmares for you, just waiting to happen.

– CHAPTER TWENTY –

SOME OTHER CRAZY DREAMERS

You, dear reader, may be "dreamers" yourselves, or you may have other "dreamers" in mind, as you read about this particular old man's dreams. I assure you, I did. I did not think of myself as being along in the world when it came to having dreams, to realizing dreams, or, sadly, not being able to make those dreams come true. I think there are a lot of us all around, and I'm guessing that we are all in one phase or another of remembering our dreams, of having dreams, of looking forward to other dreams. I must admit there is a lot of imagination involved in dreaming, but I also know there is a lot of hard work involved in actually having those dreams, in actually making those dreams come true.

Shakespeare was a dreamer, and look where his dreams took him. But . . . he was also a skilled and successful business man, who eventually was able to have built the largest house in his home town of Stratford where he retired; I'm pleased to have visited that site.

His dreams manifest themselves in his plays; many scholars think that the character of Prospero in THE TEMPEST is representative of the playwright; the character depends on his dreams of revenge (benevolent as they turn out to be) to put right, again, the wrongs to him and to his world.

Here are examples of Shakespeare's lines that address dreams:

*"I have had a most rare vision.
I have had a dream, past the wit of man to say
What dream it was."*
                    A MIDSUMMER NIGHT'S DREAM

*"For he is superstitious grown of late,
Quite from the main opinion he held once
Of fantasy, of dreams, and ceremonies."*
                            JULIUS CAESAR

*"We are such stuff
As dreams are made on . . ."*
                            THE TEMPEST

*"There are more things in heaven and earth, Horatio,
Than are dreamt of in your philosophy."*
                                HAMLET

*". . . and then they dream of love;
O'er courtiers' knees, that dream on curtsies straight;
O'er lawyers' fingers, who straight on fees;
O'er ladies' lips who straight on kisses dream;
. . . and then dreams he of another benefice;
Sometimes she driveth o'er a soldier's neck,
And then dreams he of cutting foreign throats,
Of breaches, ambuscadoes, Spanish blades,
Of healths five fathom deep . . ."*
                        ROMEO AND JULIET

One of my favorite "dreamers" from literature is Miguel de Cervantes' character, DON QUIXOTE. Cervantes was, without a doubt, a dreamer himself, who often struggled with the real world, never quite finding the successes he was looking for until late in his life. He was an avid reader and an early writer, but he put those efforts aside to join the Spanish military; he was brave and fought fiercely, and was seriously wounded. At one point, after the war, he was captured by the Turks and imprisoned (actually enslaved) for five years until he was ransomed by his family. It is not too much of a stretch to believe that he survived that imprisonment with the help of his dreams.

It is entirely possible, that the character, Don Quixote, is an avatar for the author himself. Don Quixote read way too many books on chivalry and, eventually, declared himself a knight. He set out, then with his squire, Sancho Panza, to reform the world and to revive the age of chivalry. He thinks country inns are castles, flocks of sheep are armies, convicts are wronged peasants, and windmills (remember that he tilted at windmills), are giants. His family finally had to rescue him from his efforts, from his dreams, really, and bring him home. There is a distinct difference between dreaming and reality, but for Cervantes and Don Quixote it was never quite clear which was which.

Scientists are mostly dreamers no matter how earnest and practical they seem to be on the surface; how else could they even imagine what there is out there to discover, and, then, actually find it. What about Archimedes? He was a Greek mathematician and inventor who is credited with discovering the principle that an object immersed in fluid will lose in weight an amount equal to the weight of the fluid displaced (that is now called "Archimedes' Principle"). I can't even imagine dreaming about any thing like that. It is said that the idea occurred to him in his bath as he was puzzling over how to tell a gold crown from one alloyed with silver, and as he displaced bath water. He is alleged to have leaped from his bath, shouted "Eureka!", and headed out quite naked to tell anyone who would listen about his discovery. Now, that's an awakened dreamer for you.

The greatest scientific dreamer of them all was, most certainly, Leonard daVinci. I was fortunate, while working on this memoir, to see an exhibit of the dazzling Leister Codex; it is now owned by billionaire, Bill Gates, who is kind enough to lend portions of it out to major museums for the rest of us to see. What's there in the Codex, as it is interpreted for us (those of us who can't read its backward and upside down writing) are volumes of visions, are examples of an imagination gone wild, are thousands of timeless dreams.

Musicians are dreamers; their songs express who they are and what they are looking for; first they transport themselves to other places, to other times, to other connections; then, the music is, also, meant to stimulate others (that is you and me) to dream, to feel, to try, to laugh, to cry, and/or to love.

Think of how many songs that have the word "dreams" and "dreamer" in them; I keep wanting to include some of those lyrics here. I can't afford the rights to do so, but I can list a few titles: OUT OF MY DREAMS by Richard Rodgers & Oscar Hammerstein; I DREAM OF JEANNIE by Stephen Foster; A DREAM IS A WISH YOUR HEART MAKES by Mack David, Al Hoffman, & Jerry Livingston; THE IMPOSSIBLE DREAM (from MAN OF LA MANCHA about Don Quixote, see above) by Mitch Leigh & Joe Darion; DREAM (WHEN YOU'RE FEELING BLUE) by Johnny Mercer; and YESTERDAY by Paul McCartney (who has said that he "wrote" the whole thing in a dream, and had to rush to write it down in the morning before he would forget it).

– CHAPTER TWENTY-ONE –

REALITY IS THE OTHER SIDE OF DREAMING

I'm really pretty big on reality; I'm actually quite the pragmatist; that's how I function on a day to day basis; I am not really a "dreamer." Oh, I do dream dreams, but that is not my regular way of dealing with life . . . except . . . it is . . . sometimes . . . my way of coping with the realities of life. It might just be worth our while, then, to look at a few of the realities that I live with, deal with, and have to cope with. This is not all bad; most of it is quite good; but it is just the case, as the case might be. Reality can be a good thing, too.

Let's talk about family, my most important priority. My wife is a very independent woman who is her own person, but . . . she is my soul mate, my counterpart, and we never mind that togetherness. She continues to work at a part-time job that she has held for 18 years, and which she loves. Of course, as has been mentioned before, she is a retired teacher. She has a degree in Elementary Education and in Music. She is also an excellent vocalist, having sung in and directed many church choirs, and having soloed at many a social event, wedding, or funeral. She sang at our wedding, from the back of the church, on her father's arm, just before processing; the song was "Dearest Jesus, Draw Thou Near Me". I still get chills thinking about it; it was beautiful; but I have to admit, I was the more nervous one.

We have three sons; they are all college graduates: one in Philosophy, one in Business and Economics, and one in Music Education. They were always good students for the most part, and they have always been active in school and community activities; they have made their own marks which is as it should be, and which go way beyond ours. They all are married and have varied careers; fortunately for us, they live nearby. As different as they are from one another, they are so much alike that when we all get together, they will soon be off to the side catching up, joking around, and laughing loudly, usually, as it turns out, at my expense.

Among them are our six grandchildren (two to a family); I think of them as our legacy; we love them dearly, and we try to see them as often as we can (that's one of the reasons we stay in Minnesota even in the most miserable winters). We can get to a soccer game or two, a piano recital, some rugby, a cello concert, a dance program, the BoyChoir, birthday parties, and holiday gatherings; we can have them over when their parents need to be off somewhere else; they love Grandma's cookies, and Grandpa's special ice cream cones. My collection of poems, SOUNDS FROM INSIDE ME, is dedicated to them.

We are lucky enough, to have three step-grandchildren, too; all of them (that makes nine total) get along just fine; they are all their own persons, and they are all quite fun; the ages sort of mesh together; we are sort of like our own version of "The Brady Bunch."

We aren't exactly homebodies, but we certainly don't mind being at home; we try to make wherever we live a reflection of who we are: clean, neat, comfortable, inviting, filled with plants and paintings and books and pictures of the family, with toys, and treats, and the aromas of good cooking/baking. An associate, upon entering our home, commented that it was just like a museum (we do have a lot of "stuff"), but we beg to differ; we see it more as a "nest", and a comfortable one at that.

We love going out and about as well; we love eating out, everything from fast food to buffets to brunches to course-after-course with just the right wines. We love concerts and plays and recitals and fine art; we feel comfortable in concert venues, in lavish auditoriums, in great halls, in fine theaters, in store fronts and back rooms, in school gyms, in church basements or sanctuaries, and in stunning galleries. We see and hear over 50 events a year; and . . . we also do love baseball, especially (even though it's sometimes a struggle) the <u>Minnesota Twins.</u>

– CHAPTER TWENTY-TWO –

A Dream List or Two

I'm a list maker; I've mentioned that before, and you've already seen some of them. Yes, I have to admit to it; most people who know me already know about my lists. Lists are definitely a part of these dreams; some of them are of things already accomplished; some are of things currently being worked on; some are still to come. Sometimes I even add items that are almost accomplished to certain kinds of lists, so that I can cross them off right away to encourage me to keep working them down. In fact, at one time, years ago, I was accused by a misguided friend of leaving special lists for my new wife to accomplish while I was at work; what that confused friend (who later became a dear friend) didn't know is that my wife is her own list maker; I didn't need to leave anything extra for her to do. She makes them for herself, and, most certainly, for me, as well.

When I have a project, like getting a play on the stage, or planning a vacation, or teaching a class, or starting a new job, or writing a book, I make lists, not so much outlines, not so much notes, but . . . lists. This book is pretty much drawn from the lists I made in longhand, in pencil, on narrow-ruled notepaper, in a soft-sided notebook, to get me started; I've crossed lots of things off, but most of what was there on the lists is still here, just better developed, I hope; some things have been added as I went along, and some things have been left behind.

I'll take just a paragraph to make a list, here, of some of my other lists: my best friends through the years; cities and countries I have visited; songs I used to solo on (I was a boy-tenor); vinyl Broadway show albums; some disappointments; a few of my favorite things; inventions I appreciate; and foods that I hate (in alphabetical order: asparagus, clam chowder, mushrooms, okra, oysters, squash, and wild rice).

There are two other food lists, as well, one has to do with favorite foods themselves, and one has to do with favorite places to eat those favorite foods. The first list contains things like hamburger; I don't dress it up by calling it ground beef or prime-burger, I call it hamburger, plain-old, and I like it fixed almost any which way. It is so versatile, hot dishes, tacos, loosemeat, even tartare, but there is nothing quite like the carefully and perfectly considered burger, itself, with everything on it (or almost). I was raised in the restaurant business; my dad was a trained chef, and people came from literally miles around to enjoy, to appreciate his burgers and others of his menu items; he had a carefully-protected secret for his great French fries (everybody likes bacon). He never let his customers down, even when those he had trained (such as my brother), were doing the preparing; his high standards needed to always be maintained.

I like pie, better than cake or cookies or rolls, but about the same as I like (no . . . love) donuts. My favorite pies are one-crust like pumpkin and custard and banana cream and lemon (with meringue). I'm pretty patriotic, but good old American apple pie is pretty far down on my list, and don't even mention anything with coconut to me. As for donuts, give me jelly-filled (I think of them as "Bismarks") and glazed-raised, early-morning-fresh; I once went back to visit the <u>Alamo</u>, so that I could get more of the delicious donuts served at the variety store just across the street.

Thanksgiving is my favorite holiday, because it is all about eating. I grew up with the *big* bird already in the oven in the middle of the night, so that it would be ready for a mid-day meal. Oh, the aromas in the house to wake up to on that morning. I'm pretty sure that the quality of the cooking has something to do with it; I come from a family of good cooks, but . . . I also love the camaraderie that makes it taste all that much better. In my book of poetry, I have included the following poem; you be the judge:

THE THANKS IN THANKSGIVING

The turkey, the stuffing, the gravy, the pie,
Potatoes, cranberries, fruit salad, oh, my,
Hot buttered biscuits, and chilly white wine,
The thanks in Thanksgiving are mine.

The young have come home from their work, school, and play;
Relatives gather from far, far away;
Together to pray, and together to dine,
The thanks in Thanksgiving are mine.

The weather is nicer than ever can be;
Our hearts are engladdened by all that we see;
The feelings are filling; the feelings are fine;
The thanks in Thanksgiving are mine.

Now we've come to some of my favorite places to eat, my dream places, if you will. The first place that comes to mind is the Sandpiper in Atlanta; well . . . it used to be in Atlanta; it is gone now, the victim of some new development in such a fast growing city. I loved the atmosphere, and I loved the crab-stuffed flounder; I've had it many times. All their seafood choices were extra-special; who doesn't like Mahi-Mahi? I know that's not quite fair, because lots of people have not even tried this fabulous tropical sea fish (I think of it as Hawaiian); you all really should if you ever get the chance.

I spent quite a bit of time in Atlanta; the company I worked for had a branch there, and I was the National Director of its costume operations. I saw lots of theater there, as well. One time we bought a huge costume inventory from a defunct shop, had it trucked to Atlanta, and spent several days sorting and deciding if it was worth keeping or not. The ragman got lots of it, but much of it, repaired, cleaned, and pressed went into stock all over the country to be used again and again.

It was hot, hard, dirty work, but we knew when it was quitting time and when it was time to relax, and we had some really fine dining after each full day's work. I remember going outside the city to a back-country restaurant called <u>Aunt Fanny's Cabin</u>; it was in some very old, preserved, slave quarters, quite politically incorrect by today's standards, not quite as much so at the time. The menu was traditional Southern fare; it was called out from a blackboard and chalk menu by actors/servers who were affecting a lifestyle from the past. I was quite stunned by the casual callousness of the situation, but even more so by the long lines of people out the door waiting for a table well into the evening, night after night. The food, by the way, was terrific, especially the southern-fried chicken.

Other eating-out places I have really liked were: <u>Cielito Lindo Dos</u> in Boca Raton, FL; It was our favorite Mexican restaurant when we lived there and we took many visitors to enjoy it. We loved <u>Wing City</u> in Coral Springs for the delicious and generous portions of Buffalo wings (the concept imported from up-east and which turned out to be a particular favorite of mine), and for the atmosphere where one could get a *yard* of beer that had to stand on the floor, and where one could just shuck the shells of the free peanuts and toss them under the table.

We have something of a family tradition when it comes to the <u>Lone Spur</u> (sort of a "Tex-Mex" place) in Minnetonka; we started going there after we came back from Florida as we searched this area for the perfect Buffalo wings; we found them there, and there were so many other things that became favorites; on special occasions, we try to get there where we all sort of feel we belong.

A Dream List or Two

For his high school graduation party, our oldest grandson requested that food from the <u>Lone Spur</u> be served.

These days one of our favorite places is <u>Brit's</u>, just a few blocks from our condo. On any lovely spring-to-autumn day, we can walk there, snag a table on the sidewalk along the <u>Nicollet Mall</u>, order a "sampler" (cod pieces, chicken strips, Scotch eggs), some chips, and some wine, and just take it easy, just enjoy the moment, and just watch the rest of the world go by; such sweet relaxing, such sweet eating, and such sweet dreaming.

– CHAPTER TWENTY-THREE –

WHAT IF I NEVER DREAMED OF IT AT ALL?

I certainly haven't dreamed of being or doing or having everything; I never imagined certain situations at all; some things that I never, ever dreamed of, some rather negative things, as a matter of fact, need to be shared here.

Health and wellness especially, or lack of them, come immediately to mind. For instance, I never dreamed of having Shingles, although I did know that if one had Chicken Pox, one was susceptible to them. I got mine full-force on the eve of my 50-year high school class reunion.

I had been feeling a bit poorly, and I had noticed some different-looking blemishes which were like hard scabs, and which hurt more than a usual sore; the real shock came when I woke up the morning of the reunion with blood-red eyes that hurt a lot, to say the least. It was a Saturday, so I went immediately to an urgent care unit at a large, nearby hospital; I had to wait quite a long time before being seen, but when the doctor came into the examining room, he paused, took one look at me, and proclaimed, "You've got Shingles." He had no doubt at all, and I had this feeling that he was only confirming what I had sort of thought all along. He prescribed a regimen of very expensive pills (which made me feel even sicker), and some serious resting and special care of the eyes (they are one of the most serious places to have the disease strike); so I missed the reunion, and from what I hear, I missed what was a very good dinner for which I had already paid plenty (and that made me feel even worse).

In the theater there is a way to express "Good Luck" contrarily so as not to disturb the playful spirits of the stage; that expression is "Break a leg!" Who would ever dream of actually doing It? I surely would not . . . but . . . I surely did do it.

I was directing in summer stock, and we were in "tech" week; we were practicing the light changes and the scene changes, and we were trying to get some sense of the timing and the flow of the show. At one point, in the dark, the stage-hand was unable to make the lighting change which had to do with resetting and reconnecting a floor lamp. I stopped for what I hoped was just a minute, called for lights up, and went onto the stage to show him how to make it. Once accomplished, I yelled to all, including the technician in the lighting booth, that we were going right on, so "places" and "lights out." As I was crossing downstage to some steps that went onto the floor and into the orchestra pit, the lights went out, and . . . I . . . missed the steps . . . and plunged into the concrete pit. My only thought, as I was falling, was, "This is really going to hurt!" And . . . it really did!

I yelled again, "Lights up," and we went right on. No one knew for the time being that anything untoward had happened. I, of course, was in some kind of shock, and not fully aware of how badly I had been hurt, so we just finished the act, and when we were finished, I told the cast I had fallen, just so they knew; I gave notes and schedules, and dismissed them.

There is much else that I had to contend with in the next few days, like making a fast car trip to Minneapolis to meet the composer and the sound designer for a new tape to replace the one I had destroyed when I fell, but I hobbled along on a very sore right leg, because we were opening on Thursday night; of course, I was in some kind of shock. When I finally got to the doctor, one week later, he chastised me bigtime, x-rayed the leg, discovered that I had torn all the ligaments and pulled all the muscles from the inner ankle to the back of the knee, and . . . snapped my fibula. I was too swollen to put it in a cast, so I had some sort of immobilizer for two weeks until the swelling went down, and . . . the show played on to rousing success.

I was referred to an Orthopedist, and my eventual cast was 40 pounds of fiberglass which I wore throughout the rest of the summer into the fall. I missed the <u>Twins</u> in the <u>World Series</u> except on TV, but I was sure to get to a traveling circus when it came to town; I climbed the rickety steps up the rickety bleachers using crutches and some strong assistance; I wanted to find just the right spot with a place to rest my leg and with a good view of the performances.

I remember my first outing several days after getting the cast, and after having developed an intense case of "cabin fever;" it was to the nearest <u>KFC</u> drive-through (actually in the next town) for some crispy chicken and some mashed potatoes, and a corn muffin, and a <u>Coke</u>. I just stretched out across the back seat, my accommodating wife was the perfect chauffeur, and the perfect server. I don't think <u>KFC</u> or any other fast food ever tasted so good.

I was a year recovering from that little incident. I was lucky enough not to have pins in my leg; it was a serious consideration. I had been told that I might not ever walk the same again, the bones would heal fastest and best, but the muscles, the tendons, and the ligaments were so seriously damaged, that they might not heal as well, and they would probably bother me for the rest of my life. So . . . being as strong-willed as I am . . . I did everything the doctors and the therapists told me to do to recover. It began with leg lifts no more than a half inch above the footstool where my leg was perched, slowly and painfully, again and again. I advanced from cast to immobilizer to soft wraps; I went from wheelchair to a walker to crutches to a cane: I had water therapy and heat therapy and physical therapy; it took me a good year to get somewhat back to normal.

I still have unpleasant reminders of that accident, even a sort of flashback sometimes; some physical reminders are more serious than others; I am plagued by Restless Leg Syndrome for which I take medication; some continuing discomfort seems to depend on the weather (which is a *real* thing according to my several doctors), but . . . I am proud to say, that today, no one would know that there was a time when I thought I might never walk the same again, or at all. My right leg is now shorter than my left, and my right foot is one size smaller than it was before.

I never dreamed of having four . . . count 'em . . . four . . . strokes. The first one, called "acute ischemic thalamic," happened at work. I was working as a security guard at the MIA; it was just before lunch; suddenly, my right arm just went numb, and other things in my head were not quite right. I played it down with my friends who were nearby, and I just went on with my day; I would soon be breaking for lunch. I knew, though, that something was more seriously wrong. I did not go to the doctor until the next day, and he had me transferred immediately to the emergency room of the nearest hospital.

I am not going into the details of that assessment, that confinement, the being so sort of out of it, that full-body MRI, all those tests, the addition and change in medication, the therapy . . . been there, done that . . . but I do want to mention a small remembrance of talking, through my haze, about good wine with the admitting doctor. He was apologizing for the long wait-time for a room, and I said that I'd rather be home with a "nice" glass of wine. He asked me what I liked, and I said I liked a lighter white, a Chardonnay or a Chablis; he said that they were "nice", but he suggested that red is probably somewhat better for us, because of the anti-oxidants; he liked a "nice" (there's that word again) Cabernet. What a "nice" chat we had in the middle of my *"nice" little* crisis.

I live with some residual damage especially in my nose, which always feels numb, my lips, and in my right hand and arm, which feel as if it they have fallen asleep and won't wake up no matter how hard I shake them. In this case, my motor skills were most affected; that is noticeable in my writing; I have to think to shape letters, and then I still may not be able to shape them correctly; I redo a lot of my words; I always need an eraser nearby. My writing was never much to brag about, so as it is now, we don't even want to talk about it. Oh, yes, and another thing or two, I tie my shoes as if I were just learning how, and I can barely tie a tie whenever one is needed.

I am not going into the details of my next three strokes either; they were embolic, and came as a cluster, again . . . totally out of the blue, about a year later. This time I had some sense of what was happening, so I talked to my doctor at once, and was sent, again, to the emergency room. Everything was much the same as before, and I ended up with another MRI, more tests, new medication, more therapy, etc., as well as some more invasive treatment such as a "transesophageal echocardiogram" which required me to swallow a small camera so as to be able to check the back of my heart to see if there was any damage there. Are we having fun yet?

This time, the damage was more cognitive; I work harder to remember; I struggle for a word; it takes two tries to form a thought; I have more *"senior moments."* It should be said, though, that, all in all, for what it's worth, I've done very well; I've been very lucky. Many people tell me that they would never know that I have had a stroke at all. That's the same story as with my broken leg since I can walk just fine (with the sometimes help of my cane). It seems, then, that this old man is one tough *bird*.

– CHAPTER TWENTY-FOUR –

Never Dreamed It; Couldn't Be Better

There are some things one doesn't even dream about, because there is no point of reference, nothing to prompt even daydreams or wishful thinking. I'm writing about serendipity here; you've heard about that: a capacity, a gift, for making useful or happy discoveries by chance (from THE THREE PRINCES OF SERENDIP, a Persian story about three princes who had such an ability); it's to be taken seriously, and it is not just to be taken as coincidence or good luck.

I never dreamed of, never even imagined, going to Florida to vacation or on business, let alone to live there; ah . . . but . . . serendipity led us there, and . . . we loved it. We lived there for over 6 years, and we would go back again in a so-called "New York minute;" (oops . . . I guess that's from another part of my story). I was hired for a job that was headquartered in Pompano Beach; we lived in nearby Margate, but eventually moved to Coral Springs, a planned community on the edge of the Everglades. We were less than ten miles from the beach where we ventured every chance we got; we came to love the ocean. We also loved the average temperatures, spring, summer, winter, fall, 88-92; we sort of got used to the humidity. We always carried a sweater or jacket in the car for when we needed it indoors at a mall or at a theater. No daily weather report was very necessary except in hurricane season (we were there just on the edge of Hurricane Andrew, a very scary experience, nonetheless).

We entertained many friends and relatives while we were there. My mother would come twice a year for 4-6 weeks; she liked it there, too; she especially like eating out; one time we dined at 30 different restaurants (from fast food to fine) during her stay. The beach was always a big part of what we loved, and what we shared with guests; so were the varied and terrific places to eat that we sought out, enjoyed, and shared.

I surely didn't dream of becoming a costumer; I dreamed about many other aspects of the theater, but costuming came about quite by accident.

We had moved to the suburbs, and I was looking for work. In the meantime I was substitute teaching; sometimes that wasn't so bad. One school in particular was a pure joy to go to, from the classes I got to teach, to the quality of the students, to the friendliness and helpfulness of the other teachers and staff. On the other hand, one school, which should have been a model by its location and its reputation, was a nightmare; the classrooms were not well kept up, the students were snotty and unruly, and the other teachers and staff couldn't care less that I was there. I was seriously looking for something else more satisfying and more permanent.

One day I saw a want ad in the daily paper for a "Costume Assistant"; it was a theatrical job, so it struck a chord with me. I called, at once, for an appointment; I was scheduled for the next day. I was nervous and uncertain, but I was ready for a challenge, and I needed a job; we had one toddler and a baby on the way. I need not have been nervous; everyone was most gracious, and I definitely could see the challenge. I was hired on the spot for my appropriate education, because of my teaching credentials, and for my extensive theater experience. I like to think I was also hired, in part, because I am literate, I speak clearly and well, and I present myself in a proper manner. There were just these two little quibbles: 1) I knew nothing about costuming other people's shows per se, and 2) I didn't know how to sew a stitch.

I was at that job for two years where I learned all about the costuming-from-stock business and theatrical supply in general.

The first show I ever structured and costumed by myself was A MAN FOR ALL SEASONS (elaborate, historical, elegant, Renaissance); I was proud of that effort which I researched to a fine point; it was a big success; it became the standard wardrobe plot for years after. I loved the people I worked with; they became like family; they were so creative, so energetic, and so friendly and helpful; many of them became long-standing friends.

But . . . I was a harried young dad with two small children, and the hours were long and hectic and tiring, and although I wasn't unhappy, we just thought it would be better to go back to the regular hours of teaching (even if I would have stacks of papers to correct after school, since I was an English teacher) and to having a more regular home life in a smaller town.

We had an offer that was too good to be true, which we planned to take, but . . . that school called my old school for a reference, and my old school, then, knew I was available, so . . . they made me an even better offer to return to them, and . . . I did.

I'm something of a restless person, and, after a few years, I decided I needed another change. This is going to be hard to believe, but when the costume company heard that I was again available, they called me to ask if I would be interested in coming back to them. This is going to be even harder to believe, but . . . I said that I would, if the conditions were right. They made the conditions right for me, and . . . I went back.

There are bits and pieces of this particular time in my life in other chapters; it was a big and important part. I never dreamed of it, but it couldn't have turned out better. I was there until I was hired away to go to New York; now, that's the top of the line! What more can I say?

I never dreamed of teaching outside Minnesota; I am Minnesota-born and bred; but . . . I ended up in Sheldon, Iowa. I interviewed for and was offered the job the same day I visited, so, being very practical, and not yet having heard from any of my other prospects, I signed a one-year contract. It must have been fate, because when I got home from that interview, an offer I had been waiting for was waiting for me at our postal station. Yikes, I was stuck; Yikes, was I stuck? Yikes, I decided that I was, at least, for that one year.

I repeat: it must have been fate. I used to ask in my literature classes, "What part does fate play in the life of the protagonist (the main character in a play or story)?" Fate can play a really big part; It was at that job in Iowa that I would meet the girl who became the love of my life. You see . . . the woman I would come to marry had also just signed a one-year contract to teach there as well.

We have been married over fifty years now; (I never dreamed that would happen, either). When we celebrated our 50th anniversary, the whole family gathered at our condo for drinks and hors d'oeuvres. To everyone's surprise, I had hired two horse-drawn carriages to transport all of us to a well-known and quite terrific Italian restaurant, for dinner; we were able to have a mini-tour of the nearby parks before being dropped off. After a fine dinner, served family-style, and with an elegant twin cakes anniversary dessert, I surprised the grandchildren, especially, by having a fleet of Pedi-cabs pick us up, drive us around a bit, race each other a little, and drop us off back at home. It was, to say the least, a really fun time!

The next morning, Arlis and I left for one more trip to our favorite place, New York City, of course. We had talked, often, about where we might want to go and what we might want to do. What would be really special for this milestone anniversary? It turned out to be a no-brainer; we agreed, just like that, and . . . away we went.

– CHAPTER TWENTY-FIVE –

When a Dream That Never Was Comes True

The other day, I was describing to my wife certain items in the preceding chapter. Out of the blue, she asked me, "Did you write about the fact that you *never* dreamed of *ever* getting married?"

"No, I haven't written about it, yet, but I'm going to;" and since she was correct, and I had, in fact, planned to mention it all along, here is that tale to be told.

I went from Minnesota to Sheldon, IA, to teach Senior English and Speech; Arlis came from South Dakota to Sheldon, IA, to teach Elementary Music; I had never taught before, having just graduated in the spring from the University of Minnesota in Minneapolis; Arlis had taught one year after having graduated from Southern State Teacher's College in Springfield, SD.

We were two of several single teachers who happened to land in Sheldon that year, for one reason or another; (I was hired because the Superintendent was also a U of M graduate; Arlis was hired because of a connection, since her brother had taught there some years before). We all banded together to find our own places in that small, conservative town, and to provide some social life, some entertainment, and as much camaraderie as possible.

All in all, it was not a bad place to be (except for the 99 inches of snow that winter); nor was it a difficult school year (except for the 14 days we missed because of the snow). We were dedicated to our jobs to a person, but, we were also dedicated to having fun outside of school. We traveled to nearby larger towns looking for good restaurants, for sights to see, for concerts and plays; but, mostly, we gathered at one home setting or another to barbecue, to share potluck, to have a wee drink or two, to chat earnestly, and, often, to sing around a piano or accompanied by a guitar.

On one of those occasions, I was standing at the back of the group gathered around an old, upright piano; we were singing pop songs and sentimental favorites; I'm a decent and a fairly lusty singer; at the end of a song, Arlis turned to me and commented that I had quite a nice voice; that was high praise from the music teacher; I rarely blush, but I felt something of a flush, because I really am a bit shy, and because I was truly flattered; I thanked her kindly, and we went on with a few more old favorites.

The thing about that brief discourse was that it was really the first time I had ever noticed her. I was in the High School where there were others I had noticed, and she was in the Elementary School, and, actually, traveled to three different locations in the district; I just didn't get to see her all that much. It was also true that just a few days before, she had gotten her hair restyled from a rather severe look to a more fresh and flowing one (she says that, when driving back to town from the stylist, truckers even whistled at her). Whatever . . . I finally noticed her, and then I made much more of an effort to see her, and to talk to her, and to get together with her on other occasions than just with the group.

My housemates and I were planning a big Christmas party before we all went our separate ways for the holiday itself. We were inviting all the singles with whom we got together regularly and a few of the young marrieds who had also become our friends. We made special invitations (a green scroll tied with a red ribbon and a red bell); we secured good wine (Iowa was a dry state with state-owned, permit-required, liquor stores); we planned a complete holiday menu (turkey and all the trimmings and plum pudding); with the help of our school's set designer, we decorated beautifully the apartment of one of our single friends; and we arranged for preferred seating. My one request was that Arlis would be seated next to me; unnnh, hmmmm, ohhhh; what? Please, just do it for me. They did, and she was, and the rest is . . . well . . . history, as they say.

So . . . here we are today. We dated throughout the winter; we were engaged at Easter time; we were married in the summer. The green scroll invitation is framed and hangs out each Christmas; the red bell and ribbon hang as an ornament on our Christmas tree. We have even been featured in a major newspaper's article about our favorite and long-standing Christmas treasure.

– CHAPTER TWENTY-SIX –

Was It All Just a Dream?

Sometimes, in looking back, a lot of what has gone on seems pretty much like a dream, or, rather, a series of dreams. I've had several *"lives,"* so to speak, some very different from the others, and as one fades, and I change, and another takes over, each previous one is remembered much the same way one remembers a dream. Some of the facts are quite vivid, even colorful; others are sort of fuzzy; we want to hang on to what we can; but so many are hazy, unclear, distant, and some just can't be clearly recalled at all.

What we dreamed for ourselves for our lives may or may not have come to pass. Other things that we never dreamed at all may have made up significant parts of our lives. We, probably, remember some of them warmly, but there are others we would, more than likely, just as soon forget, or, at least, keep in some sort of perspective, sort of in their place.

As the years go by, and memory fades, or totally fails us, there is that haziness about what we do recall, and about what we can recall. Some things get extra emphasis; we remember what we want to remember, what we especially liked, and others don't even seem true, are not all that exciting or fun, and just don't even make the cut.

I often say to myself, "Did that really happen?" "Was that really me involved in that situation?" "Am I really sure of what I think I remember?" "Was this some kind of dream?" I'm not sure, always, that others even believe me when I tell them the facts of what really was.

I'm happy to say that my memory is pretty good for my age, maybe even for any age; I pride myself on that, just as my mother did; she was quite physically weak for the last years of her life, but her mind was as sharp as a tack until the very end, not just at recalling the past, but being right up to the minute on what was going on around her and even keeping up with the news; she remembered all the kids' and grandkids' birthdays, and she would call them and play a happy birthday song for them from a small recording machine; she remembered all the rules of the several games we played, and . . . she managed her own several medications.

I'm blessed by not having had my memory that much affected by my four strokes and the subsequent and significant variety of medications. I do work at remembering; I challenge myself; I keep up with the news regularly (I'm something of a news "junkie," actually); I ask questions; let it be said that I love JEOPARDY (please, put your answer in the form of a question), and I try to watch it daily; years ago we were actually at a double taping of the show when it was still in New York. I make it a point to seek answers and opinions and discussions and arguments. I listen carefully; I like to hear; I like to know what others have to say, and I truly care about it; and . . . I write things down . . . a lot.

I don't mean to imply that any of us just wander through life in a dream; I'm just referring to how we recall it; what are the facts after the facts? Was it all really real? Was it all we ever wanted it to be? How do we remember it? Why do we even try? Maybe, we come to like the idea of that sort of dream-like quality that makes up our past; maybe it helps us to manage, to understand, and to appreciate our lives. There is a softness, a pleasantness, a comfort, in the *haze* of our memories.

– EPILOGUE –

Hey, Dreamer, It's Time to Wake Up

I am something of a dichotomy; I'm not really a dreamer per se; I'm really more practical than that, something of a pragmatist. A few years ago, a woman in Minneapolis got this idea for what she called a "minimal memoir;" the proposition was whether or not one's life could be summed up in just six words. It was more of a party game than anything else, but it was a particular chance to think about oneself and to express what that thinking was; it did require some time and effort. I think you can still find out more about it at "6wordsmpls.com."

Arlis and I tried it, and we were surprised at how much thought we gave to it, how much we discussed it, and, actually, how difficult it turned out to be; we had a good time, though, a sort of thoughtful, meaningful, rather interesting time together.

Here are the results: Arlis wrote: "Wife, Mom, Grandma! Singer, Dancer, Dreamer!" She is all of those things! I wrote: "Say about him that he tried!" Notice that I was the practical one, the realistic one, and, I assure you, I was very earnest; I want others to remember me for that; if I were to have an inscription on my tombstone, it would be, "He tried!" As it turns out, we both plan to be cremated and find that forever rest in the Columbarium at our church; no inscriptions beyond names and dates are permitted.

I'm bifurcated (I love that word; I love words in general); there are, at least, two sides to me. I like it that way; things can be more interesting, and I really like *interesting*; maybe, the only thing I like more, one of my necessities, is *choice*, and it was my choice to pursue this memoir from the standpoint of my visions, my hopes, my wishes, and my dreams.

I'm not so different from you; we all have dreams, but we all have that practical side of life, that reality, that which, most of the time, works for us, but sometimes gets in the way. I tried to not let that be the case, although facts are facts are facts, and life is life is life. "We are such stuff as dreams are made on, and our little life is rounded with a sleep;" (that's from Shakespeare's THE TEMPEST, one of my favorite plays).

I've told a lot of stories in the preceding pages; I've revealed more of myself than I usually do. I've adjusted and arranged. I've bragged and bemoaned. I've careened and/or careered (whichever you prefer). I've dived down and dug deep. I've tossed and twisted and torn. If I'm not completely satisfied, I have no one to blame but myself, but . . . I'm pretty satisfied, and I'm ready to wake up from what was this ongoing dream.

Of course, there is more to tell; I've been pretty selective; I've tried to stick to the *"conceit"* that is my dreams; I've tried to find the interesting, the exciting, the different, special, and particular elements of this old man's life. I did leave out a lot of the negative stuff; I've had enough of that. It is true, that what one finds worth telling (from an insider's point of view) may just not be all that worth reading (from an outsider's perspective). I hope that's not the case here.

Perhaps, though, I need to wrap it all up with something that I am relatively sure will be interesting and memorable, and maybe even exciting:

When I arrived in New York to begin my new job there, alone this time and really quite nervous, I took a shuttle from LaGuardia to Midtown, got settled in my Westside apartment, and decided to walk out on what was such a lovely fall day. I planned to scout out the neighborhood, to get a Sunday <u>New York Times</u>, to have some good Italian food with a nice Chianti for dinner, and, then, get back to the <u>Esplanade</u> for some rest, some relaxation, and to ready myself for a busy new day, and/or a week, and/or the months ahead.

I was headed south on Seventh Avenue to where it crosses Broadway; I still felt pretty much a visitor, a tourist, a proverbial "hick from the sticks," when I spotted a huge billboard above <u>Times Square</u>. <u>Budweiser</u> was using a particular advertising campaign and slogan at the time, and just then, when I needed something to encourage me and to make me feel welcome, that big billboard read, "New York, this BUD'S for you!"

I never even dreamed it quite like that; what an impact; I realized that there I was, for real, in the ♥ of one of my dreams.

I've definitely moved on from that particular dream, and I'm quite comfortable with that, so I guess I should probably rub my eyes, pinch myself (hard), drink some more dark, strong coffee, and totally wake up. Ah, yes, good readers, "Good morning to you."

I am pretty much "up"; I will usually be "at 'em"; I think that I can, now, get on with whatever other parts of this lifetime may still be left.

For whatever it's worth, though, if anyone out there is still interested, especially after all these many words, and all these many pages, what I finally have left to say is *"THIS* BUD'S FOR YOU!" Thanks for your attention.

– CODA –

A LONG, LONG TRAIL

There's a long, long trail a-winding
Into the land of my dreams,
Where the nightingales are singing,
And the white moon beams;

There's a long, long night a-waiting
Until my dreams all come true,
Till the day when I'll be going down
That long, long trail with you.

—Stoddard King (1889-1933)

NOTE: A CODA, in some pieces of music, a final section that adds dramatic energy to the work as a whole, usually through intensified rhythmic activity; an additional section at the end of a text, e.g., a literary work or speech, that is not necessary to its structure but gives additional information.

---MICROSOFT *ENCARTA* COLLEGE DICTIONARY

– ACKNOWLEDGEMENTS –

ARLIS PRESCOTT . . . My wife, of course; I thank her the most; if it is all about me, it is, also, all about her; we truly completely agree that we are one.

RICK PRESCOTT . . . Our oldest son, who is a computer "wiz;" he has been the most helpful in getting this book ready for publication (as he has been with the previous ones); if I can't do something that I want done or that I need done (and that's a lot of things), he most surely can and will be able to do it.

ANN WOOD . . . A good friend, who actually suggested and encouraged the possibility of this book; my thanks to her.

PAUL THEROUX . . . One of my favorite writers whose travel books and novels delight me (I've read most of them), and whose style gives me hints of how to do it right; I think I use a very similar style; I hope I use it as right as he does, and as well.